Primary 3B
Preface

Primary Mathematics Intensive Practice is a series of 12 books written to provide challenging supplementary material for Singapore's Primary Mathematics,

The primary objective of this series of books is to help students generate greater interest in mathematics and gain more confidence in solving mathematical problems. To achieve this, special features are incorporated in the series.

SPECIAL FEATURES

Topical Review
Enables students of mixed abilities to be exposed to a good variety of questions which are of varying levels of difficulty so as to help them develop a better understanding of mathematical concepts and their applications.

Mid-Year or End-Of-Year Review
Provides students with a good review that summarizes the topics learned in Primary Mathematics.

Take the Challenge!
Deepens students' mathematical concepts and helps develop their mathematical reasoning and higher-order thinking skills as they practice their problem-solving strategies.

More Challenging Problems
Stimulate students' interest through challenging and thought-provoking problems which encourage them to think critically and creatively as they apply their knowledge and experience in solving these problems.

Why this Series?
Students will find this series of books a good complement and supplement to the Primary Mathematics textbooks and workbooks. The comprehensive coverage certainly makes this series a valuable resource for teachers, parents and tutors.

It is hoped that the special features in this series of books will inspire and spur young people to achieve better mathematical competency and greater mathematics problem-solving skills.

Published by
SingaporeMath.com Inc
404 Beavercreek Road #225
Oregon City, OR 97045
U.S.A.
E-mail: customerservice@singaporemath.com
www.singaporemath.com

First published 2004
Reprinted 2005

ISBN 1-932906-05-3

Printed in Singapore

Our special thanks to Jenny Hoerst for her assistance in editing the U.S. edition of
Primary Mathematics Intensive Practice.

Primary 3B
Contents

Topic 1: Addition and Subtraction (Mental Calculation)

Add Tens and Ones Strategy

Example: Add 58 and 35.
            58 + 30 = 88
            88 + 5 = 93

35 = 30 + 5

1. Add using "add tens and ones strategy".

   (a) 67 + 29 = _____   (b) 42 + 81 = _____

   (c) 36 + 57 = _____   (d) 85 + 69 = _____

   (e) 93 + 18 = _____   (f) 44 + 102 = _____

   (g) 24 + 77 = _____   (h) 50 + 88 = _____

   (i) 69 + 63 = _____   (j) 46 + 92 = _____

2. Find the sum of (a) 63 and 34,
                    (b) 123 and 56.

Make Nearest Tens Strategy

Example: Add 58 and 35.
            58 + 2 = 60
            60 + 33 = 93

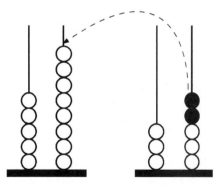

5 tens 8 ones   3 tens 5 ones

1

3. Add using "make nearest tens strategy".

(a) 71 + 29 = _____

(b) 43 + 67 = _____

(c) 19 + 84 = _____

(d) 25 + 76 = _____

(e) 52 + 89 = _____

(f) 34 + 48 = _____

(g) 78 + 14 = _____

(h) 67 + 24 = _____

(i) 56 + 33 = _____

(j) 91 + 26 = _____

4. What number is (a) 25 more than 95, _____

(b) 36 more than 145? _____

Add Hundred Strategy

Example: Add 245 and 99.
             245 = 244 + 1
             244 + 100 = 344

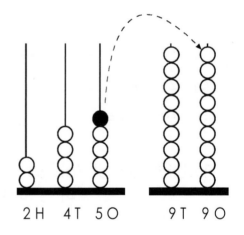

2 H   4 T   5 O   9 T   9 O

5. Add using "add hundred strategy".

(a) 75 + 98 = _____

(b) 45 + 99 = _____

(c) 65 + 97 = _____

(d) 35 + 96 = _____

(e) 52 + 98 = _____

(f) 86 + 99 = _____

(g) 78 + 98 = _____

(h) 26 + 97 = _____

(i) 16 + 96 = _____

(j) 47 + 97 = _____

Subtract Tens and Ones Strategy

Example: Subtract 35 from 60.
             $60 - 30 = 30$
             $30 - 5 = 25$

I remember
$30 + 5 = 35$

6. Subtract using "subtract tens and ones strategy".

(a) $67 - 23 =$ _____   (b) $82 - 41 =$ _____

(c) $56 - 31 =$ _____   (d) $87 - 55 =$ _____

(e) $100 - 25 =$ _____   (f) $44 - 12 =$ _____

(g) $97 - 45 =$ _____   (h) $49 - 31 =$ _____

(i) $72 - 23 =$ _____   (j) $93 - 54 =$ _____

7. Find the difference between (a) 90 and 34, _____

(b) 74 and 26. _____

8. The difference between two numbers is 53. If the bigger number is 100, what is the smaller number?

Subtract from Nearest Tens Strategy

$60 = 40 + 20$

Example: Subtract 35 from 60.
             $40 - 35 = 5$
             $20 + 5 = 25$

9. Subtract using "subtract from nearest tens strategy".

(a) $70 - 27 =$ _____   (b) $90 - 15 =$ _____

(c) $50 - 24 =$ _____   (d) $60 - 48 =$ _____

(e) $80 - 57 =$ _____   (f) $30 - 19 =$ _____

(g) $40 - 28 =$ _____   (h) $70 - 46 =$ _____

(i) $80 - 36 =$ _____   (j) $100 - 72 =$ _____

10. What number is (a) 51 less than 90, _____

    (b) 18 less than 100? _____

11. The sum of two numbers is 200. One of the numbers is 128. What is the other number?

Subtract from Hundred Strategy

Example: Subtract 99 from 245.
245 = 145 + 100
100 − 99 = 1
145 + 1 = 146

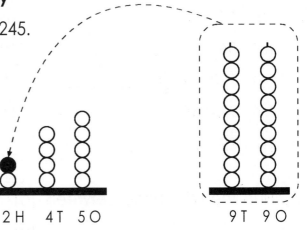

2 H   4 T   5 O   9 T   9 O

12. Subtract using "subtract from hundred strategy".

    (a) 145 − 98 = _____   (b) 236 − 99 = _____

    (c) 164 − 97 = _____   (d) 130 − 96 = _____

    (e) 251 − 98 = _____   (f) 186 − 99 = _____

    (g) 178 − 98 = _____   (h) 224 − 97 = _____

    (i) 153 − 96 = _____   (j) 242 − 97 = _____

Multiply by Tens and Hundreds Strategy

Example: 5 tens × 3 = 15 tens
                       = 150

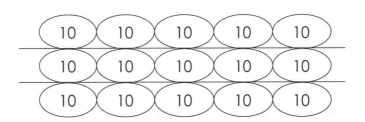

13. Multiply using "multiply by tens and hundreds strategy".

    (a) 6 tens × 3 = _____   (b) 9 tens × 5 = _____

    (c) 4 tens × 8 = _____   (d) 50 × 6 = _____

    (e) 80 × 9 = _____   (f) 30 × 4 = _____

    (g) 5 hundreds × 3 = _____

    (h) 7 hundreds × 4 = _____

    (i) 2 hundreds × 9 = _____

    (j) 300 × 5 = _____   (k) 700 × 3 = _____

    (l) 800 × 4 = _____

14. Find the product of (a) 70 and 7,
                           (b) 100 and 12.

Divide by Tens and Hundreds Strategy

Example: 15 tens ÷ 5 = 3 tens = 30

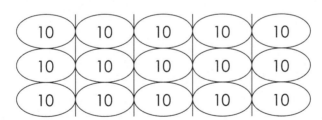

15. Divide using "divide by tens and hundreds strategy".

    (a) 12 tens ÷ 3 = _____   (b) 8 tens ÷ 2 = _____

    (c) 16 tens ÷ 8 = _____   (d) 50 ÷ 5 = _____

    (e) 180 ÷ 6 = _____   (f) 120 ÷ 4 = _____

    (g) 3 hundreds ÷ 3 = _____

    (h) 12 hundreds ÷ 6 = _____

    (i) 20 hundreds ÷ 5 = _____

    (j) 300 ÷ 6 = _____   (k) 2700 ÷ 9 = _____

    (l) 2800 ÷ 7 = _____

WORD PROBLEMS

1. Arnold has 100 stamps. Howard has 20 stamps less than Arnold. How many stamps do Howard and Arnold have altogether?

2. Mr. Green had 165 apples. He threw away 39 rotten apples and sold the remaining good ones. How many apples did he sell?

3. Nicholas saved $60 a month. Julie saved 8 times as much as Nicholas in a month. How much did Julie save in a month?

4. Alicia had 30 cards. Clementine had twice as many cards as Alicia. If Evelyn had 160 cards, how many cards did all three have?

5. Mr. Cooper has 4 times as much money as his son. If Mr. Cooper has $800, how much money do both of them have?

6. Rosie collected 110 red beads, 68 blue beads and 72 green beads. She used them to form 5 chains of equal length. How many beads did she use to form each chain?

7. Daniel and Paula have 5000 coins altogether. If Daniel has 4 times as many coins as Paula, how many coins does Daniel have?

8. There are 600 pages in a storybook. Billy read 3 such storybooks.
   (a) How many pages did he read in total?
   (b) If Billy read the 3 books in 9 days, how many pages did he read in a day?

9. A box contains 100 pens. In the box, there are 46 blue pens, 34 black pens and the rest are red pens. How many red pens are there in 9 such boxes?

10. Sylvia has $47. Mariam has $13 more than Sylvia. Lauren has $8 less than Mariam.
    (a) How much money does Mariam have?
    (b) What is the total amount of money?

Take the Challenge!

Solve these problems using mental calculation strategies you have just learned.

1. Potatoes were sold at 10 for $3. A grocer had 3000 potatoes in his store. If he sold all of them, how much money would he collect?

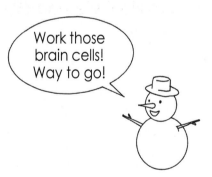

Work those brain cells! Way to go!

2. Uncle Lionel picked 800 apples from his orchard. He gave away 80 of them and packed the rest into bags of 9 each.
   (a) How many such bags of apples did he get?
   (b) If he sold each bag for $6, how much money did he collect?

3. Maria gave her friends 3 pieces of candy each. She kept 9 pieces of candy for herself. How many friends received candy from Maria if she had 69 pieces of candy at first?

Topic 2: Length

1. Fill in each blank with the correct estimated length.

   (a) Length of my palm _____

   94 ft

   (b) Distance round the school field _____

   5 in.

   (c) Thickness of a dictionary _____

   12 ft

   (d) Length of the basketball court _____

   50 m

   (e) Length of an Olympic-sized _____
   swimming pool

   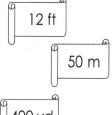
   400 yd

   (f) Length of a motorcar _____

   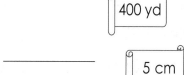
   5 cm

2. Convert the following into centimeters.

   (a) 1 m 85 cm = _____ cm   (b) 6 m 45 cm = _____ cm

   (c) 9 m 27 cm = _____ cm   (d) 15 m 8 cm = _____ cm

   (e) 26 m 17 cm = _____ cm   (f) 10 m 3 cm = _____ cm

3. Convert the following into meters and centimeters.

   (a) 167 cm = _____ m _____ cm

   (b) 800 cm = _____ m _____ cm

   (c) 409 cm = _____ m _____ cm

   (d) 75 cm = _____ m _____ cm

(e) 1529 cm = _____ m _____ cm

(f) 1206 cm = _____ m _____ cm

4. Convert the following into feet.

   (a) 6 yd = _____ ft   (b) 62 yd = _____ ft

   (c) 8 yd 1 ft = _____ ft   (d) 23 yd 2 ft = _____ ft

   (e) 12 yd 1 ft = _____ ft   (f) 100 yd 2 ft = _____ ft

5. Convert the following into yards and feet.

   (a) 7 ft = _____ yd _____ ft

   (b) 80 ft = _____ yd _____ ft

   (c) 49 ft = _____ yd _____ ft

   (d) 75 ft = _____ yd _____ ft

   (e) 129 ft = _____ yd _____ ft

   (f) 106 ft = _____ yd _____ ft

6. Convert the following into inches.

   (a) 1 ft 10 in. = _____ in.   (b) 6 ft 4 in. = _____ in.

   (c) 8 ft 3 in. = _____ in.   (d) 3 ft 8 in. = _____ in.

   (e) 2 ft 11 in. = _____ in.   (f) 10 ft 3 in. = _____ in.

7. Convert the following into feet and inches.

   (a) 10 in. = _____ ft _____ in.

   (b) 25 in. = _____ ft _____ in.

   (c) 40 in. = _____ ft _____ in.

   (d) 48 in. = _____ ft _____ in.

8. Compare the lengths using "shorter than", "equal to" or "longer than".

(a) 189 cm is _____ 1 m 89 cm.

(b) 12 m 5 cm is _____ 125 cm.

(c) 404 cm is _____ 4 m 44 cm.

(d) 658 cm is _____ 65 m 8 cm.

(e) 20 m 4 cm is _____ 204 cm.

(f) 4056 cm is _____ 4 m 56 cm.

(g) 14 in. is _____ 1 ft.

(h) 6 yd 2 ft is _____ 20 ft.

(i) 32 in. is _____ 1 yd.

(j) 100 ft is _____ 32 yd 2 ft.

(k) 1 cm is _____ 1 in.

(l) 36 in. is _____ 1 m.

9. Write the longest and the shortest length for each set.

	Longest	Shortest
(a) 1 m 54 cm, 10 m 45 cm, 5 m 41 cm, 1 m 45 cm	_____	_____
(b) 1889 cm, 188 m 9 cm, 1 m 889 cm, 18 m, 98 cm	_____	_____
(c) 2 m 2 cm, 2002 cm, 20 m, 20 cm, 1999 cm	_____	_____
(d) 605 cm, 5 m 65 cm, 6 m 50 cm, 60 m 5 cm	_____	_____
(e) 39 in., 4 ft, 1 yd, 28 in., 3 ft 4 in, $\frac{1}{2}$ yd	_____	_____

10. Add and subtract in compound units.

    (a) 2 m 45 cm + 1 m 15 cm = _____ m _____ cm

    (b) 3 m 69 cm + 1 m 21 cm = _____ m _____ cm

    (c) 5 m 42 cm + 4 m 68 cm = _____ m _____ cm

    (d) 15 m 84 cm + 2 m 98 cm = _____ m _____ cm

    (e) 31 m 26 cm + 10 m 87 cm = _____ m _____ cm

    (f) 1 m 56 cm – 45 cm = _____ m _____ cm

    (g) 3 m – 1 m 42 cm = _____ m _____ cm

    (h) 6 m 63 cm – 4 m 55 cm = _____ m _____ cm

    (i) 10 m 78 cm – 3 m 56 cm = _____ m _____ cm

    (j) 85 m 50 cm – 32 m 78 cm = _____ m _____ cm

11. Add and subtract in compound units.

    (a) 2 yd 2 ft + 1 yd 2 ft = _____ yd _____ ft

    (b) 32 yd 1 ft + 67 yd 2 ft = _____ yd _____ ft

    (c) 12 yd 2 ft + 9 yd 2 ft = _____ yd _____ ft

    (d) 5 ft 2 in. + 4 ft 6 in. = _____ ft _____ in.

    (e) 15 ft 8 in. + 22 ft 9 in. = _____ ft _____ in.

    (f) 31 ft 7 in. + 10 ft 5 in. = _____ ft _____ in.

    (g) 45 ft 3 in. + 12 ft 8 in. = _____ ft _____ in.

    (h) 1 yd 2 ft – 2 ft = _____ yd _____ ft

    (i) 32 yd – 7 yd 2 ft = _____ yd _____ ft

    (j) 6 yd – 10 ft = _____ yd _____ ft

    (k) 10 ft 8 in. – 3 ft 6 in. = _____ ft _____ in.

    (l) 8 ft 5 in. – 2 ft 8 in. = _____ ft _____ in.

    (m) 85 ft. 4 in. – 7 ft 7 in. = _____ ft _____ in.

    (n) 100 ft. – 27 in. = _____ ft _____ in.

12. Convert the following into meters.

(a) 1 km 650 m = _____ m   (b) 4 km 108 m = _____ m

(c) 9 km 115 m = _____ m   (d) 8 km 28 m = _____ m

(e) 6 km 7 m = _____ m   (f) 8 km 453 m = _____ m

13. Convert the following into kilometers and meters.

(a) 9107 m = _____ km _____ m

(b) 6500 m = _____ km _____ m

(c) 5047 m = _____ km _____ m

(d) 6006 m = _____ km _____ m

14. Compare the lengths using "shorter than", "equal to" or "longer than".

(a) 1139 m is _____ 1 km 39 m

(b) 1205 m is _____ 1 km 205 m

(c) 7704 m is _____ 7 km 44 m

(d) 6 km 8 m is _____ 6080 m

(e) 2 km 408 m _____ 2048 m

(f) 4056 m _____ 4 km 56 m

(g) 1008 m _____ 1 km 80 m

(h) 1 mi _____ 2580 ft

(i) 7 mi _____ 7 km

15. Add and subtract in compound units.

(a)	km	m	(b)	km	m	(c)	km	m
	3	241		8	867		3	975
+	2	723	−	5	256	+	1	764

(d)	km	m	(e)	km	m	(f)	km	m
	8	321		2	34		6	75
−	3	479	+	5	248	−	1	309

12. Use the diagram below to answer the following questions.

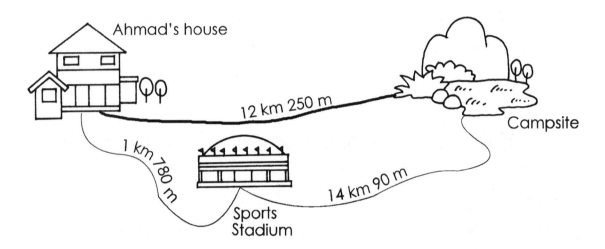

(a) Ahmad's house is _____ m away from the Sports Stadium.

(b) If Ahmad is at the Sports Stadium, he is _____ km _____ m from the Campsite.

(c) If Ahmad meets his classmates at the Sports Stadium before going to the Campsite together, he must travel _____ km _____ m.

(d) Ahmad decides to go to the Campsite on his own from home. He will travel _____ km _____ m less than if he goes with his classmates.

(e) The Campsite is _____ m nearer to Ahmad's house than the Sports Stadium.

16

WORD PROBLEMS

1. Tim has 3 routes to choose from when he travels from his house to town. Look at the diagram below. Which is the shortest route?

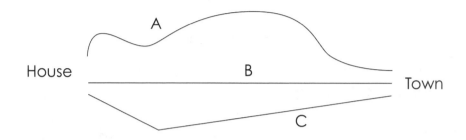

___B___ is the shortest route.

2. Clara is 3 ft 6 in. tall and her sister, Jessie, is 50 in. tall. What is the difference in their height?

$$\begin{array}{r} 50 \\ -42 \\ \hline 8\,\text{in} \end{array}$$

3. Look at the two lines A and B drawn below.

$$\begin{array}{r} 3\,\text{m} \\ -1\tfrac{1}{2}\text{m} \\ \hline 1\tfrac{1}{2}\,\text{m} \end{array}$$

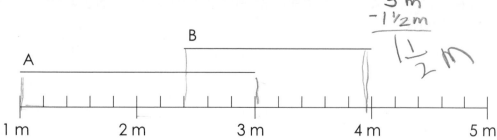

Line A is ___150___ (cm) longer than Line B.

4. The distance around a running track is 428 m. Paul ran round the track 3 times. What is the total distance Paul ran? Give your answer in km and m.

1284 m

$\frac{1284}{1000}$ = 1.284 km

5. Mimi bought 7 m of ribbon. She used 128 cm to tie round a gift box and another 89 cm to tie a bow on top of the box. What was the length of ribbon left?

100 cm = 1 m

6. Eddie must jog a total distance of 3 mi. If he has already jogged 2 mi 1750 yd, how far more has he to go? Give your answer in yards.

7. Mr. Yee drove 8 km 405 m from Town A to Town B. He had to drive another 6 km 800 m before reaching Town C. How far is Town C from Town A?

8. The length of a wooden plank is 6 m 25 cm. The length of a bamboo stick is 3 m 68 cm shorter than the wooden plank. What is the total length of the wooden plank and the bamboo stick?

9. A rope is 15 ft 6 in. long. It is 2 ft 8 in. longer than another rope. How long are both ropes altogether?

```
  '15                32 in           '1'86 in
 × 12                                 154 in
 ─────                               ─────────
   3 0                               (340 in)
 1 5
 ──────
 1 80 in                      028.333  = 28⅓ ft
 +  6 in                   12 │ 340.00
 ──────────                     -24
 (186 in)                      ──────
 - 32 in                        10 0
 ──────────                     -9 6
 (154 in)                      ──────
                                 40
                                -36
```

10. Mark had a string 23 ft 4 in. long He used 75 in. of the string to tie a package and cut the remaining string into 5 equal pieces. What was the length of each smaller piece of string?

Take the Challenge!

1. Rapunzel tried to escape from the castle where she was kept prisoner. She found 5 pieces of curtains each 225 cm long and tied them together to use as a long rope. Any two adjacent pieces of curtains were tied together by a knot. Each knot used 15 cm of each of the two ends. How long was the rope Rapunzel made?

   (*Hint*: Draw a diagram.)

   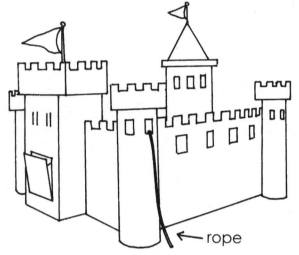

   ← rope

2. Roger, Harry, George and Mark stand in a straight line as shown in the line-up below, starting with the shortest on the left to the tallest on the right. Roger is 2nd man to the right of George. George is 3rd man to the left of Mark.

   If Harry is shorter than Roger, Mark is taller than George, and George is shorter than Harry, who is the tallest?

   $H < R$ $G < H < R$
   $M > G$
   $G < H$

20

Topic 3: Weight

1. Match the estimated weight to the correct item.

(a) A school backpack

(b) A can of soup

(c) An average-sized man

(d) A medium-sized watermelon

(e) A plastic bag of 10 quarters

(f) 8 adults in an elevator

4 kg 200 g
2 oz
5 kg
1000 lb
305 g
160 lb

2. Check the weighing scale to find out how heavy each item is.

(a)

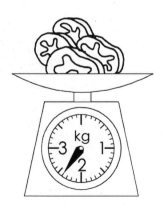

_____ kg _____ g

(b)

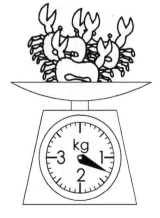

_____ kg _____ g

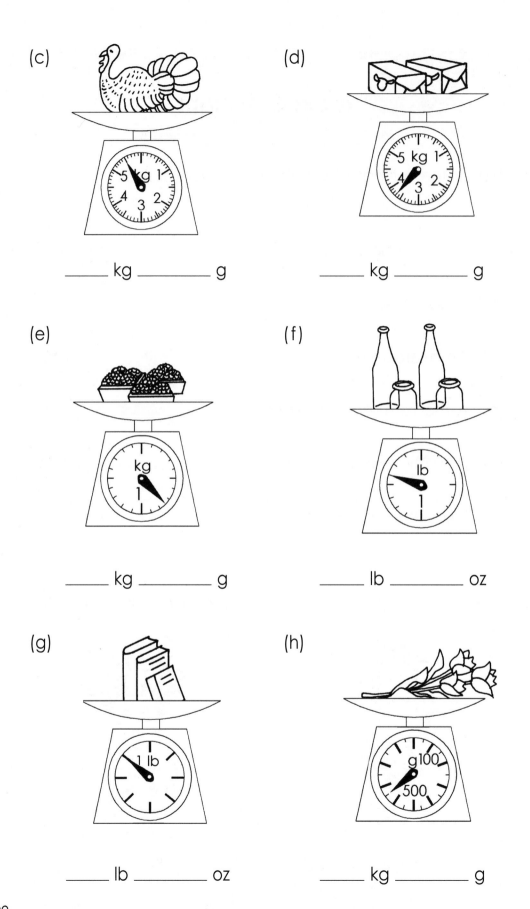

(c) _____ kg _____ g

(d) _____ kg _____ g

(e) _____ kg _____ g

(f) _____ lb _____ oz

(g) _____ lb _____ oz

(h) _____ kg _____ g

3. Convert the following into grams.

    (a) 1 kg 672 g = _____ g   (b) 4 kg 809 g = _____ g

    (c) 7 kg 53 g = _____ g   (d) 1 kg 22 g = _____ g

    (e) 6 kg 8 g = _____ g   (f) 3 kg 104 g = _____ g

4. Convert into kilograms and grams.

    (a) 940 g = _____ kg _____ g

    (b) 1058 g = _____ kg _____ g

    (c) 4307 g = _____ kg _____ g

    (d) 3148 g = _____ kg _____ g

    (e) 9435 g = _____ kg _____ g

    (f) 8006 g = _____ kg _____ g

5. Convert the following into ounces.

    (a) 2 lb = _____ oz   (b) 1 lb 8 oz = _____ oz

    (c) 4 lb 12 oz = _____ oz   (d) 2 lb 3 oz = _____ oz

    (e) 6 lb 11 oz = _____ oz   (f) 10 lb 10 oz = _____ oz

6. Convert into pounds and ounces.

    (a) 12 oz = _____ lb _____ oz

    (b) 20 oz = _____ lb _____ oz

    (c) 36 oz = _____ lb _____ oz

    (d) 10 oz = _____ lb _____ oz

7. Circle [O] the heaviest and cross [×] out the lightest.

   (a) 5 kg 850 g,   508 g,   8005 g,   5 kg 580 g

   (b) 2500 g,   2 kg 50 g,   2225 g,   2 kg 5 g

   (c) 9900 g,   10 kg,   9 kg 999 g,   9 kg 99 g

   (d) 1 kg 97 g,   1079 g,   971 g,   1 kg 971 g

   (e) 1 lb 4 oz,   18 oz,   36 oz,   2 lb

8. Compare and fill in the blanks.

   (a)
   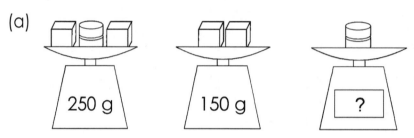

   _____

   (b)
   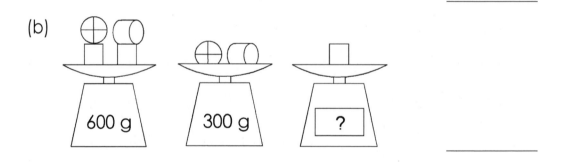

   _____

   (c)
   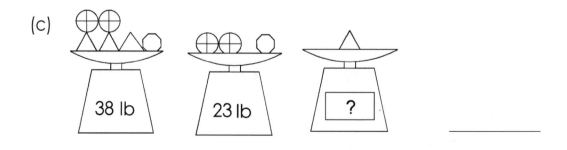

   _____

24

(d)

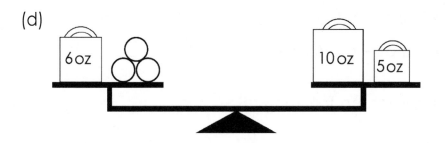

Weight of each ◯ is _____ oz.

(e)

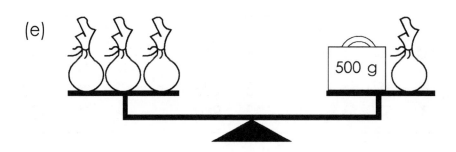

Weight of one coin bag is _____ g.

9. Add and subtract in compound units.

   (a) 2 kg 450 g + 150 g = _____ kg _____ g

   (b) 5 kg 425 g + 1 kg 380 g = _____ kg _____ g

   (c) 4 kg 85 g + 2 kg 380 g = _____ kg _____ g

   (d) 3 kg 760 g – 350 g = _____ kg _____ g

   (e) 2 kg 850 g – 1 kg 425 g = _____ kg _____ g

   (f) 6 kg 830 g – 4 kg 550 g = _____ kg _____ g

10. Add and subtract in compound units.

   (a) 2 lb 10 oz + 15 oz = _____ lb _____ oz

   (b) 5 lb 8 oz + 1 lb 11 oz = _____ lb _____ oz

   (c) 4 lb 3 oz + 21 lb 13 oz = _____ lb _____ oz

   (d) 3 lb 7 oz – 10 oz = _____ lb _____ oz

(e)   2 lb 3 oz – 1 lb 5 oz = _____ lb _____ oz

(f)   21 lb 15 oz – 7 lb 6 oz = _____ lb _____ oz

11.   Add or subtract the following.

(a)
kg	g
3	445
+ 2	825

(b)
kg	g
8	150
– 4	290

(c)
kg	g
3	975
+ 1	50

(d)
kg	g
8	320
– 3	575

(e)
kg	g
5	230
+ 3	980

(f)
kg	g
4	70
– 1	485

12.   Look at the diagrams below and fill in the blanks.

1 lb 3 oz   16 lb 12 oz   33 oz

(a)   The bowl of fruit is _____ oz lighter than the bag of food.

(b)   The shopping cart is _____ lb _____ oz heavier than the bag of food.

(c)   The total weight of all 3 items is _____ lb _____ oz.

WORD PROBLEMS

1. A box of sugar weighs 5 kg. If the empty box weighs 500 g, what is the weight of the sugar in the box?

2. A basket with 3 bags of flour in it weighs 1050 g. If each bag of flour weighs 300 g, how much does the empty basket weigh?

3. Mr. Larson weighs 132 lb. He is 3 times as heavy as his daughter, Evelyn. What is the total weight of Mr. Larson and Evelyn?

4. The total weight of John, Jack and Jimmy is 358 lb. John and Jack weigh the same while Jimmy weighs 150 lb. How much does John weigh?

5. Look at the diagram below.

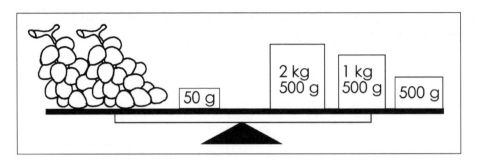

How heavy are the 2 bunches of grapes?
Give your answer in grams.

6. The weight of 3 mangoes is 1200 g. The total weight of 2 mangoes and 7 plums is 1 kg 500 g. How much heavier is a mango than a plum?

7. Mother used 2 lb 5 oz of flour to bake a cake and another 14 oz of flour to make some cookies. She found that she still had some flour left over. If Mother had 6 lb 8 oz of flour at first, how much flour did she have left?

8. At the market, 3 kg of prawns were sold for $45. 5 kg of crabs cost $90. Auntie Chong bought only 1 kg of prawns and 1 kg of crabs. How much did she pay for them?

9. A can of beans weighs 287 g. Mrs. Kwan buys a carton that contains half a dozen cans of beans. How much does the carton of beans weigh? Give your answer in kg and g.

10. William weighs 94 lb. He is half as heavy as his father, Mr. Tay. Mr. Tay weighs 4 times as much as his daughter, Mandy. How much does Mandy weigh?

Take the Challenge!

1. Four friends want to find out who is the heaviest among them.
Clarissa is lighter than Abby but heavier than Davina.
Betty is heavier than Abby.
Can you guess who is the heaviest?

2. Study the two diagrams carefully.

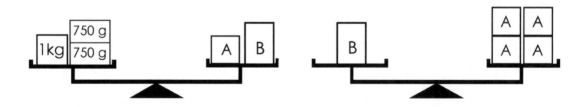

What is the weight of A in grams?

Topic 4: Capacity

1. How much can these contain? Draw a line to match the correct answer.

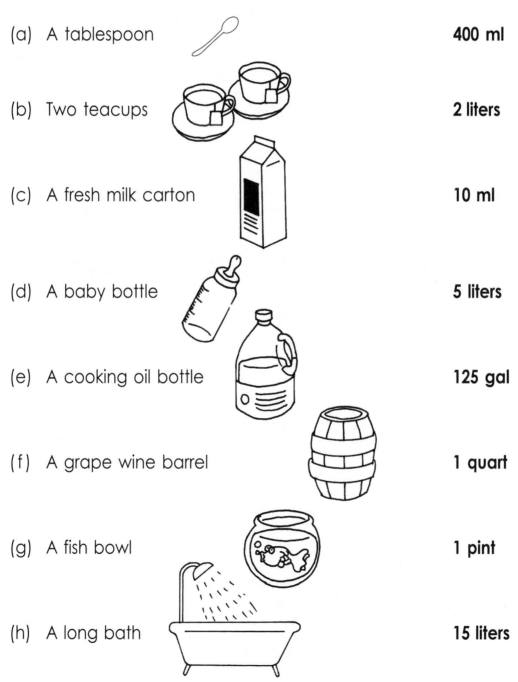

(a) A tablespoon   **400 ml**

(b) Two teacups   **2 liters**

(c) A fresh milk carton   **10 ml**

(d) A baby bottle   **5 liters**

(e) A cooking oil bottle   **125 gal**

(f) A grape wine barrel   **1 quart**

(g) A fish bowl   **1 pint**

(h) A long bath   **15 liters**

2. Find the amount of water in each container.

    (a) 5 beakers of water are needed to fill up a 1-liter measuring jug.

       Amount of water in each beaker is _____ ml.

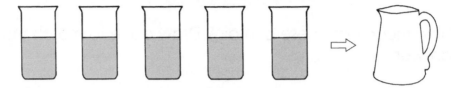

    (b) Mother used a 2-quart pot to make coffee for her guests. The pot of coffee can serve 8 coffee cups.

       Amount of coffee in each cup is _____ c.

    (c) Dr. Menderly mixed some potion in a flask and poured it into five 50-ml test-tubes.

       Amount of potion in the flask is _____ ml.

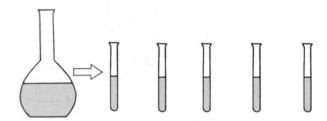

    (d) Gretel fills the cauldron with water from 20 buckets. Each bucket contains 3 quarts of water.

       Amount of water in the cauldron is _____ gal.

3. What is the amount of water in each beaker?
   Shade the boxes that contain the answers. Read the words in the unshaded boxes to form a saying.

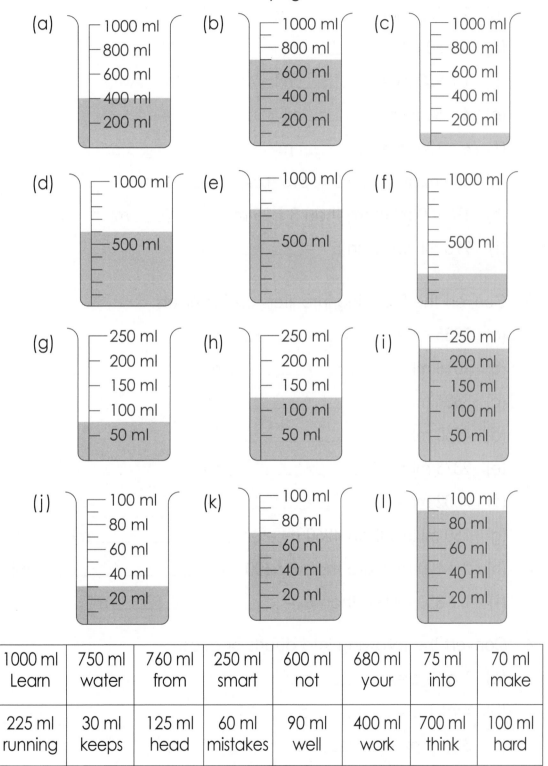

1000 ml Learn	750 ml water	760 ml from	250 ml smart	600 ml not	680 ml your	75 ml into	70 ml make
225 ml running	30 ml keeps	125 ml head	60 ml mistakes	90 ml well	400 ml work	700 ml think	100 ml hard

4. Convert the following into milliliters.

   (a) 1 ℓ 600 ml = _____ ml

   (b) 2 ℓ 755 ml = _____ ml

   (c) 3 ℓ 50 ml = _____ ml

   (d) 1 ℓ 950 ml = _____ ml

   (e) 4 ℓ 80 ml = _____ ml

   (f) 6 ℓ 105 ml = _____ ml

   (g) 200 ml less than 2 ℓ 815 ml = _____ ml

   (h) 1 ℓ 100 ml more than 3 ℓ 25 ml = _____ ml

   (i) 995 ml less than 5 ℓ = _____ ml

5. Convert the following into liters and milliliters.

   (a) 1835 ml = _____ ℓ _____ ml

   (b) 1018 ml = _____ ℓ _____ ml

   (c) 3607 ml = _____ ℓ _____ ml

   (d) 4560 ml = _____ ℓ _____ ml

   (e) 2375 ml = _____ ℓ _____ ml

   (f) 7002 ml = _____ ℓ _____ ml

   (g) 150 ml less than 4250 ml = _____ ℓ _____ ml

   (h) 2 ℓ 120 ml more than 2 ℓ 600 ml = _____ ℓ _____ ml

   (i) 1 ℓ 850 ml less than 6 = _____ ℓ _____ ml

6. Convert the following into quarts or cups.

   (a) 1 qt 3 c = _____ c

   (b) 4 pt 1 c = _____ c

   (c) 3 qt 1 pt = _____ c

(d) 1 gal = _____ c

(e) 2 gal 3 qt = _____ c

(f) 4 gal 2 qt = _____ qt

(g) 3 gal 2 pt = _____ qt

(h) 3 qt less than 12 gal = _____ qt

(i) 8 c more than 7 gal = _____ qt

7. Convert the following into the given units.

(a) 7 qt = _____ gal _____ qt

(b) 24 c = _____ gal _____ qt

(c) 9 c = _____ pt _____ c

(d) 14 c = _____ qt _____ pt

(e) 45 c = _____ qt _____ c

(f) 71 pt = _____ qt _____ pt

(g) 50 pt = _____ gal _____ qt

(h) 5 qt more than 2 gal 1 qt = _____ gal _____ qt

(i) 3 c less than 3 gal = _____ qt _____ c

8. Add and subtract in compound units.

(a) 2 ℓ 75 ml + 550 ml = _____ ℓ _____ ml

(b) 3 ℓ 123 ml + 2 ℓ 37 ml = _____ ℓ _____ ml

(c) 5 ℓ 22 ml + 2 ℓ 456 ml = _____ ℓ _____ ml

(d) 3 ℓ 540 ml – 350 ml = _____ ℓ _____ ml

(e) 4 ℓ 950 ml – 3 ℓ 720 ml = _____ ℓ _____ ml

(f) 8 ℓ 900 ml – 5 ℓ 750 ml = _____ ℓ _____ ml

9. Add or subtract the following.

(a)	ℓ	ml	(b)	ℓ	ml	(c)	ℓ	ml
	3	50		6	75		4	695
+ 2		850	− 5		200	+ 4		635

(d)	ℓ	ml	(e)	ℓ	ml	(f)	ℓ	ml
	7	300		1	275		10	20
− 2		524	+ 5		589	− 4		886

10. Add and subtract in compound units.

(a) 3 qt + 3 qt = _____ gal _____ qt

(b) 4 gal 2 qt + 13 gal 3 qt = _____ gal _____ qt

(c) 142 gal 1 qt + 457 gal 3 qt = _____ gal _____ qt

(d) 3 pt + 2 gal 6 pt = _____ gal _____ pt

(e) 4 qt 2 c + 7 qt = _____ qt _____ c

(f) 2 qt 1 pt + 4 qt 3 c = _____ qt _____ c

(g) 3 gal – 3 qt = _____ gal _____ qt

(h) 7 gal 1 qt – 3 gal 3 qt = _____ gal _____ qt

(i) 89 gal – 25 qt = _____ gal _____ qt

(j) 4 pt – 1 c = _____ pt _____ c

(k) 6 qt 2 c – 4 qt 3 c = _____ qt _____ c

(l) 6 qt 1 pt – 2 qt 3 c = _____ qt _____ c

11. Look at the pictures and answer the questions below.

1 ℓ 500 ml

150 m

2 ℓ 450 ml

(a) Tea in a full teapot can fill _____ wine glasses.

(b) There is _____ ml more wine in the bottle than tea in the teapot.

(c) The amount of liquid in the 3 containers is _____ ℓ _____ ml.

WORD PROBLEMS

1. 3 similar flasks contain 870 ml of water. A beaker contains 378 ml of water. What is the total amount of water in 1 flask and 1 beaker?

2. A toy watering can has 5 c of water. A bucket contains 5 times as much water as the toy watering can. How much water is in both containers? Give your answer in quarts and cups.

3. Mrs. Lewis had 5 bottles of cooking oil. Each bottle contained 2 liters of oil. After 3 months she found that she had 3 ℓ 650 ml of cooking oil left. How much cooking oil did she use in 3 months?

4. Mark has a fish tank at home. The tank can contain 60 gallons of water. This is 8 times the amount of water in a smaller fish tank. How much water is in the smaller fish tank? Give your answer in gallons and quarts.

5. Look at the diagrams below.

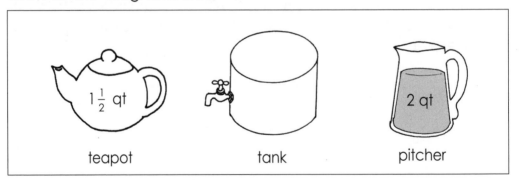

| teapot | tank | pitcher |

4 teapots and 10 pitchers of water is poured into the empty tank. How much water is in the tank?

6. Mrs. Lana bought 6 cartons of orange juice from the supermarket. Each carton contained 985 ml of orange juice. Her children drank half a liter of orange juice daily from Monday to Sunday. How much orange juice did she have left at the end of the week?

7. A pitcher contains 2 quarts of water. The water in 3 such pitchers is poured into a bucket. How many gallons of water is in a tank if the water in 8 such buckets is poured into it?

8. A 3-liter jug was empty at first. Maurice poured 2 mugs of root beer into the jug. If each mug contained 385 ml of root beer, how many more milliliters of root beer must he pour into the jug to fill it to the brim?

9. Stanley bought five 2-quart bottles of soda pop for a party. After the party, he still had one and a half bottles of soda pop left. How much soda pop did Stanley and his friends drink?

10. A drink-stall vendor sells a 250-ml cup of iced lemon tea for $1. At the end of a day, she sold 80 liters of iced lemon tea. How much money did she collect?

Take the Challenge!

1. ABC Bottling Factory invented a new machine that could fill 300 bottles of soft drink in 1 minute. Each bottle contained $\frac{1}{2}$ quarts of soft drink.
   (a) How many bottles of soft drink could the machine fill in half an hour?

   (b) How many quarts of soft drink would be needed to fill all those bottles in half an hour?

2. Container C has one and a half times the amount of water in Container B. The total amount of water in Container B and Container C is 1500 ml. If Container A has 200 ml of water, how many milliliters of water does Container A and B have altogether? (*Hint*: Draw a model.)

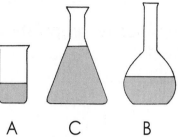

A   C   B

3. A tank can hold 30 gallons of water. It is already filled with 25 gallons of water. My sister tries to fill it with another 10 gallons of water but finds water overflowing from it. How much water overflows?

30 gal

4. Mother is going to bake a chocolate cake. The recipe requires 2 c of buttermilk. Mother wants to bake 3 such cakes. How many quart cartons of buttermilk must she buy?

Topic 5: Graphs

1. The picture graph shows the food eaten by Hungry Ogre in a week.

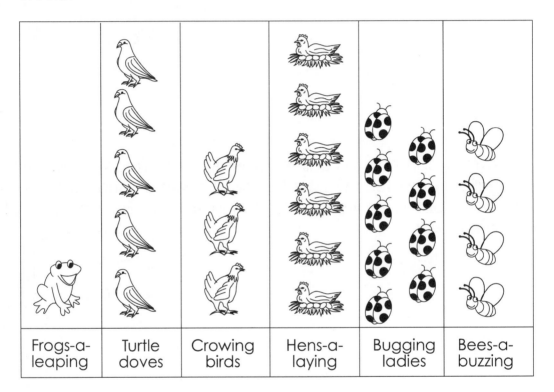

| Frogs-a-leaping | Turtle doves | Crowing birds | Hens-a-laying | Bugging ladies | Bees-a-buzzing |

(a) Hungry Ogre ate _____ times as many bees-a-buzzing as frogs-a-leaping.

(b) He ate _____ times the number of bugging ladies as crowing birds.

(c) Each hen laid 3 eggs before it was eaten. Hungry Ogre had _____ eggs for breakfast that week.

(d) Hungry Ogre ate _____ birds altogether.

(e) He ate _____ more bird(s) than insects.

2. The picture graph shows the number of animals in Cutey pet shop.

Clarice visited the pet shop and counted these animals:

10 hamsters	9 guinea pigs	14 puppies
10 rabbits	4 mice	7 kittens

(a) Complete the picture graph below. Each ◇ stands for 2 animals.

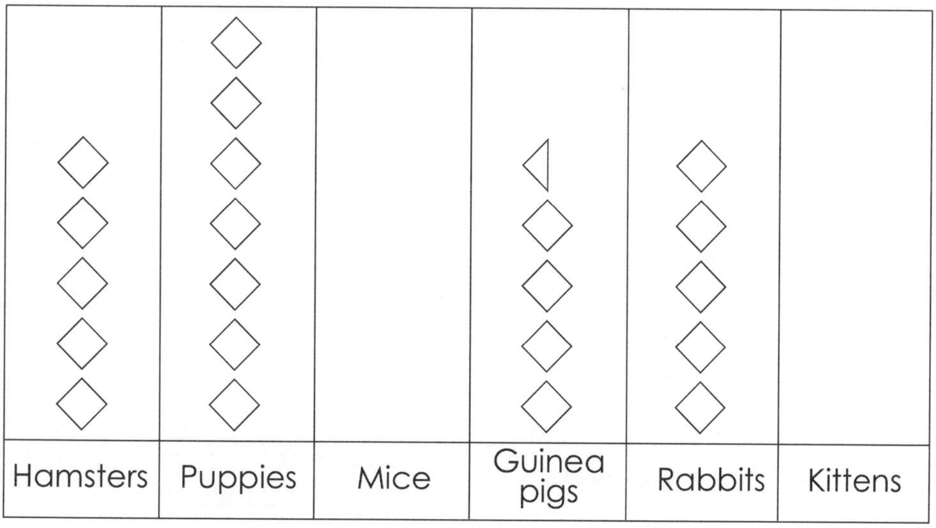

Hamsters	Puppies	Mice	Guinea pigs	Rabbits	Kittens
◇◇◇◇◇	◇◇◇◇◇◇◇		◁◇◇◇◇	◇◇◇◇◇	

(b) The number of puppies is _____ times the number of kittens.

(c) If another 10 rabbits are brought into the pet shop, then the number of rabbits becomes _____ times the number of mice.

(d) Looking at the number of animals in the pet shop, which do you think is the most popular pet? _____

(e) If 4 hamsters share a cage, how many cages are needed to keep all of them? _____

(f) A guinea pig is sold for $238. How much money will be collected if all the guinea pigs are sold? _____

(g) 2 rabbits eat about 500 g of carrots each day. How many kilograms of carrots do all the rabbits eat each day? _____

43

3. The picture graph below shows the number of items Mother has in her cabinet.

Forks	Spoons	Knives	Dinner plates	Soup bowls	Water glasses

Mother is inviting 10 friends for dinner this Saturday. Help her to find out the number of items needed. (Do not forget to include Father and Mother.)

(a) Are there enough forks and spoons? _____ (Yes or No)

(b) How many pairs of fork and spoon are needed for all the people? _____

(c) Mother found that she needs _____ more knife/knives.

(d) She has to buy 6 more dinner plates. If one dinner plate costs $8, how much does she pay? _____

(e) Mother decides to borrow some soup bowls from her neighbour. How many does she have to borrow? _____

(f) There are more than enough water glasses. How many more?

_____

4. The following graph shows the number of pages of a storybook 5 children read in a week.

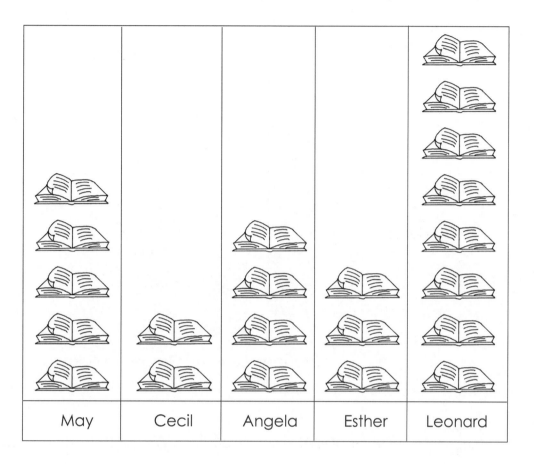

| May | Cecil | Angela | Esther | Leonard |

Each 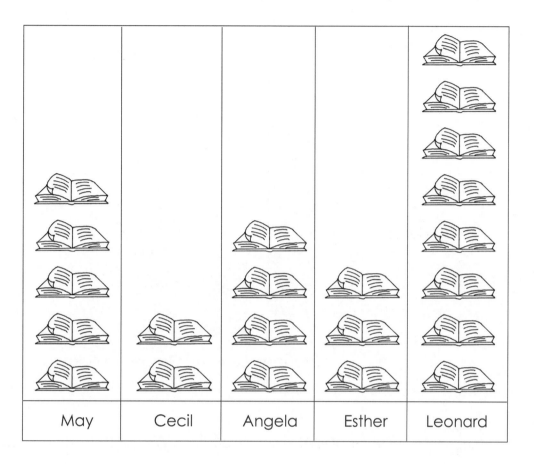 stands for 9 pages of the storybook.

(a) May read _____ pages in a week.

(b) Esther read _____ pages less than May in a week.

(c) _____ read the most number of pages of the storybook.

(d) _____ was the slowest reader.

(e) Leonard read 4 times as many pages as _____.

(f) _____ and _____ together read the same number of pages as May.

5. The following graph shows the 4 different types of fruit juice which some third grade students like to drink.

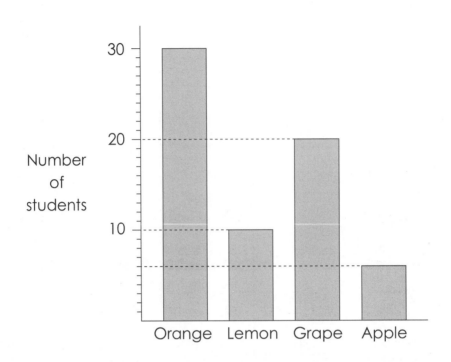

(a) How many students like to drink apple juice? _____.

(b) The most popular fruit juice is _____.

(c) _____ more students like to drink grape juice than apple juice.

(d) How many students are there altogether? _____

(e) The fruit juice that most students do not like is _____.

(f) _____ students do not drink lemon and grape juice.

(g) The number of students who like orange juice is three times the number of students who like _____.

6. The graph shows the grades earned by a group of students on a test.

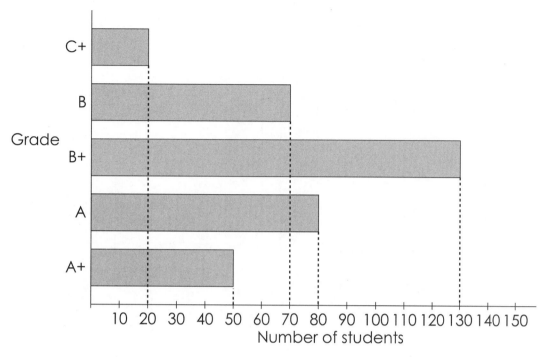

(a) Most of the students earned a _____.

(b) Only _____ students earned an A.

(c) There are _____ more students who earned a B than a C+.

(d) 80 fewer students earned a _____ than a _____.

(e) There are _____ students who earn an A and above.

(f) _____ students took the test and earned a grade.

(g) A total of 360 students took the test but those who did not complete the test were not graded. How many students were not graded? _____

7. The graph below shows the number of ceramic pots produced by a factory for the last 6 months.

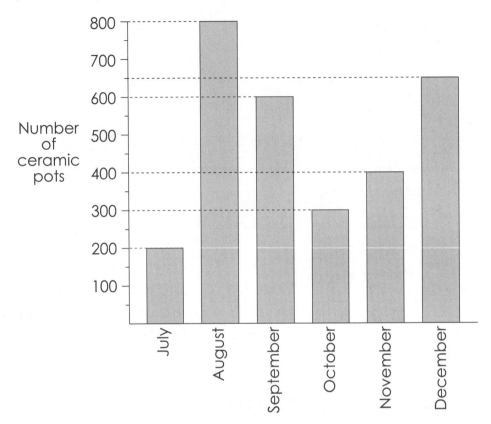

(a) The highest number of ceramic pots was produced in _____ and the lowest number in _____.

(b) _____ fewer ceramic pots were produced in July than in August and December together.

(c) If 5 pots were packed into a carton, how many cartons were used in August? _____

(d) During a sale at the factory in October, 10 pots were sold for $88. How much money did the factory collect in that sale if all the pots were sold? _____

(e) 35 pots were damaged in September. How many good pots were left for sale? _____

Take the Challenge!

1. Some children were asked to name their favorite cafeteria food in school. The information is given in the box. Draw a simple bar graph to show the information.

Hot dog	25
Spaghetti	105
Hamburger	85
Pizza	60

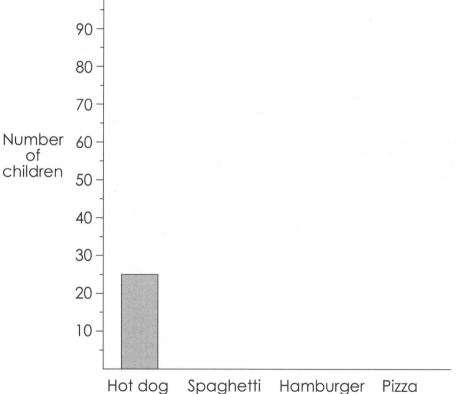

2. A group of 420 students in Novel School was asked to choose their favorite pastime. Twice as many students chose 'Play Computer Games' as 'Surf the Net'. 30 fewer students chose 'Watch TV' than 'Play Computer Games'. 175 students chose either 'Listen to Music' or 'Play Computer Games'. Ten fewer chose 'Talk on Phone' than 'Listen to Music'. 60 students chose 'Surf the Net'. The remaining students chose 'Reading'. Illustrate the given information on a bar graph.

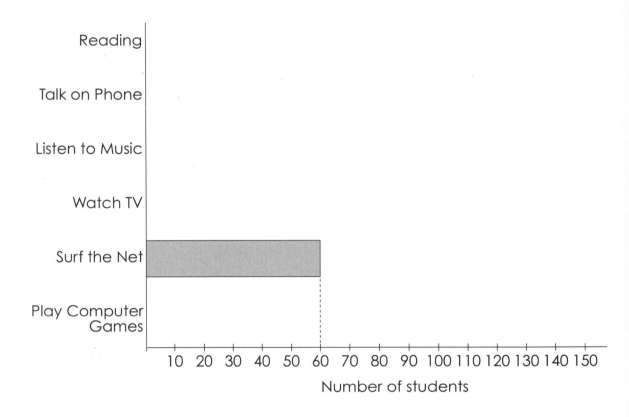

Topic 6: Fractions

1. Draw a line to match the part that has been cut from the whole on the left column and fill in the missing fractions in the boxes. One part has been done for you.

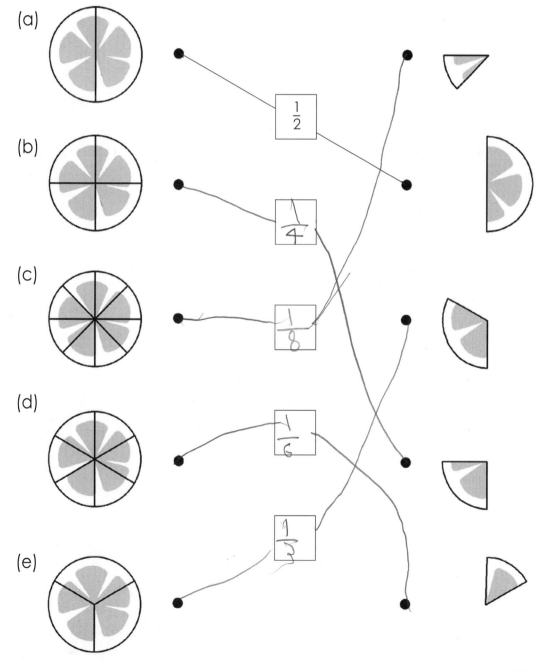

(a)

(b)

(c)

(d)

(e)

$\frac{1}{2}$

$\frac{1}{4}$

$\frac{1}{8}$

$\frac{1}{6}$

$\frac{1}{3}$

2. What fraction of the figure is
   (i) shaded,
   (ii) unshaded?

(a)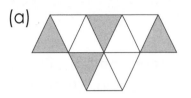

(i) $\dfrac{4}{10}$

(ii) $\dfrac{6}{10}$

(b)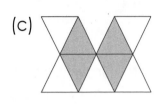

(i) $\dfrac{3}{8}$

(ii) $\dfrac{5}{8}$

(c)

(i) $\dfrac{4}{9}$

(ii) $\dfrac{5}{9}$

(d)

(i) $\dfrac{2}{8}$

(ii) $\dfrac{6}{8}$

(e)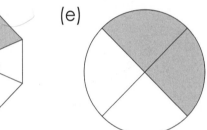

(i) $\dfrac{2}{4}$

(ii) $\dfrac{2}{4}$

(f)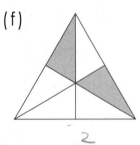

(i) $\dfrac{2}{6}$

(ii) $\dfrac{4}{6}$

(g)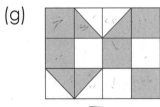

(i) $\dfrac{7}{12}$

(ii) $\dfrac{5}{12}$

(h)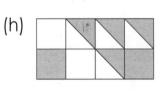

(i) $\dfrac{4}{8}$

(ii) $\dfrac{4}{8}$

(i)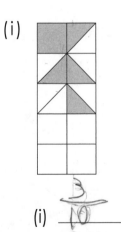

(i) $\dfrac{3}{10}$

(ii) $\dfrac{7}{10}$

3. In each figure in Question 2, the sum of the shaded parts and the unshaded parts makes _A Whole_ .

4. Work out the number of equal parts in each whole figure and write the correct fraction for each of the following.

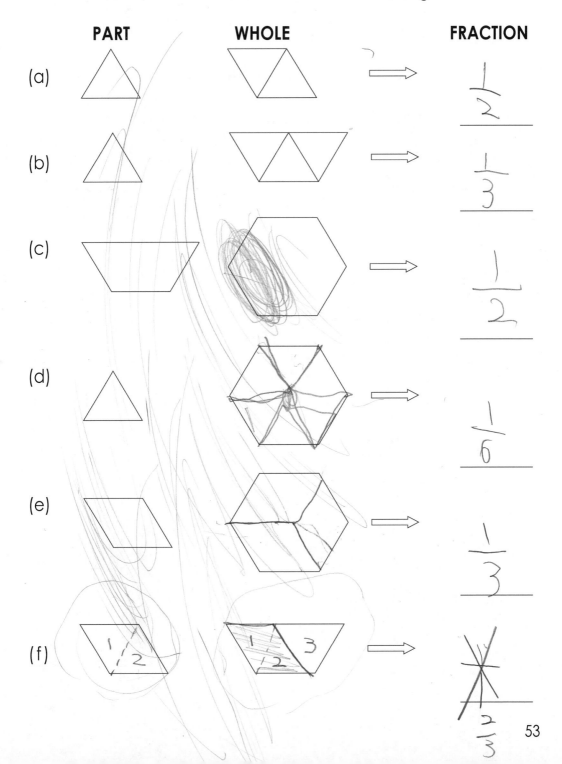

PART	WHOLE	FRACTION
(a)		$\frac{1}{2}$
(b)		$\frac{1}{3}$
(c)		$\frac{1}{2}$
(d)		$\frac{1}{6}$
(e)		$\frac{1}{3}$
(f)		$\frac{2}{3}$

5. Color each figure to show the given fraction.

(a)
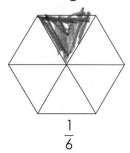
$\dfrac{1}{6}$

(b)
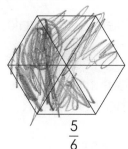
$\dfrac{5}{6}$

(c)
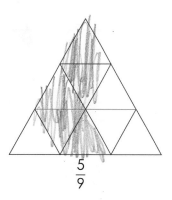
$\dfrac{5}{9}$

(d)
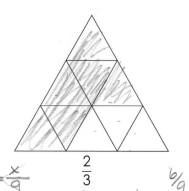
$\dfrac{2}{3}$

$\dfrac{2}{3} = \dfrac{x}{9}$

$3x = 18 \qquad x = 6$

$6/9 = 2/3$

(e)
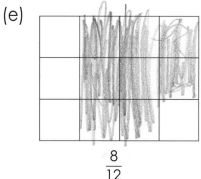
$\dfrac{8}{12}$

(f)
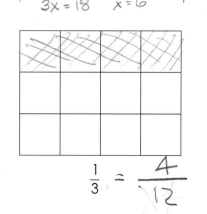
$\dfrac{1}{3} = \dfrac{4}{12}$

(g)
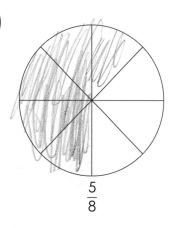
$\dfrac{5}{8}$

(h)
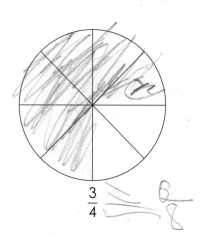
$\dfrac{3}{4}$

$= \dfrac{6}{8}$

6. Match each blank to the correct answer with a line. Each line passes through a letter. The first one has been done for you.

(a) $\frac{1}{3}$ is greater than _____ •

(b) $\frac{3}{8}$ is smaller than _____ •

(c) $\frac{3}{7}$ + _____ = 1 whole •

(d) _____ is smaller than $\frac{1}{6}$ •

(e) $\frac{7}{12}$ and $\frac{5}{12}$ make _____ •

(f) There are five _____s in a whole •

(g) $\frac{2}{9}$ + _____ + $\frac{3}{9}$ make 1 whole •

(h) $\frac{5}{11}$ is a bigger fraction than _____ •

(i) _____ is 1 equal part more than $\frac{4}{9}$ •

(j) 1 whole is the same as _____ •

(A) (O) (R) (C) (U) (I) (N) (T) (F) ('S)

• $\frac{4}{7}$

• $\frac{5}{12}$

• $\frac{1}{7}$

• 1 whole

• $\frac{3}{4}$

• $\frac{1}{8}$

• $\frac{5}{9}$

• $\frac{1}{5}$

• $\frac{6}{6}$

• $\frac{4}{9}$

(k)

Write the letters that follows each question number. The first one has been done for you.

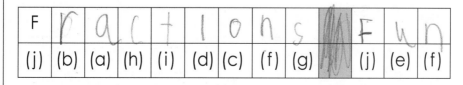

F	r	a	c	t	i	o	n	s	M	F	u	n
(j)	(b)	(a)	(h)	(i)	(d)	(c)	(f)	(g)		(j)	(e)	(f)

7. Which of the following fractions has the greatest value?

(a) $\frac{1}{9}$, $\frac{1}{5}$, $\frac{1}{12}$, $\frac{1}{6}$ _____

(b) $\frac{2}{9}$, $\frac{7}{9}$, $\frac{5}{9}$, $\frac{8}{9}$ _____

8. Which of the following fractions has the smallest value?

(a) $\frac{1}{2}$, $\frac{1}{6}$, $\frac{1}{3}$, $\frac{1}{11}$ _____

(b) $\frac{3}{6}$, $\frac{3}{7}$, $\frac{3}{8}$, $\frac{3}{4}$ _____

9. Arrange the fractions from the smallest to the largest.

(a) $\frac{1}{9}$, $\frac{1}{5}$, $\frac{1}{12}$ _____

(b) $\frac{4}{8}$, $\frac{4}{11}$, $\frac{4}{5}$ _____

(c) $\frac{2}{5}$, $\frac{3}{3}$, $\frac{2}{10}$ _____

10. Arrange the fractions from the greatest to the smallest.

(a) $\frac{1}{6}$, $\frac{1}{3}$, $\frac{1}{11}$ _____

(b) $\frac{7}{9}$, $\frac{3}{9}$, $\frac{6}{9}$ _____

(c) $\frac{3}{7}$, $\frac{3}{10}$, $\frac{3}{3}$ _____

11. Color the correct number of parts below to show some ways you can color to give the same fraction.

(a) $\frac{1}{2}$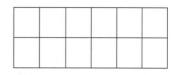

(b) $\frac{1}{4}$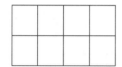

(c) $\frac{1}{3}$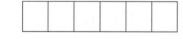

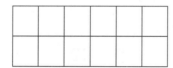

(d) $\frac{3}{4}$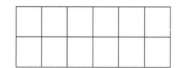

(e) $\frac{2}{3}$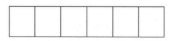

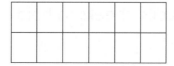

12. Choose the correct answer and write its letter above the question number in the box below to find out the riddle. The first one has been done for you.

(a) $\frac{2}{3} = \frac{\boxed{}}{9}$

(A) 3   (C) 6   (K) 4   (E) 2

(b) $\frac{4}{8} = \frac{2}{\boxed{}}$

(F) 5   (A) 8   (H) 4   (E) 1

(c) $\frac{4}{12} = \frac{\boxed{}}{3}$

(I) 1   (P) 2   (E) 3   (N) 4

(d) $\frac{5}{6} = \frac{10}{\boxed{}}$

(F) 7   (A) 8   (P) 12   (M) 10

(e) $\frac{3}{6} = \frac{\boxed{}}{12}$

(U) 4   (M) 6   (Y) 12   (C) 1

(f) $\frac{\boxed{}}{5} = \frac{8}{10}$

(U) 4   (Z) 5   (K) 2   (U) 11

(g) $\frac{\boxed{}}{8} = \frac{9}{24}$

(V) 6   (G) 2   (N) 3   (Z) 4

(h) $\frac{6}{21} = \frac{2}{\boxed{}}$

(H) 2   (A) 3   (W) 8   (K) 7

A mammal that puffs out its cheeks to hold its food.							
C	h	i	p	m	u	n	k
(a)	(b)	(c)	(d)	(e)	(f)	(g)	(h)

WORD PROBLEMS

1. What fraction of the flowers is not in the vase?

$\frac{2}{5}$

2. Molly cut her birthday cake into 10 equal slices. She and her 6 friends each ate one slice. What fraction of the cake was left?

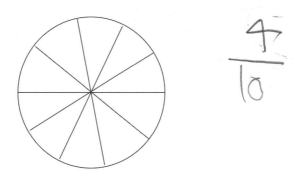

$\frac{4}{10}$

3. Alan and Mark shared a bar of chocolate.

    Alan ate $\frac{2}{9}$ of the bar of chocolate and Mark ate $\frac{4}{9}$ of it. What fraction of the bar of chocolate was eaten?

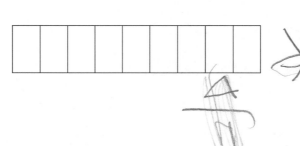

$\frac{3}{9}$

4. Mother cuts a pizza into 12 pieces. Six children share the pizza equally. How many pieces can each child get?

5. A watermelon was cut into 12 pieces. Kelly ate 1 piece and her sister took 4 pieces. What fraction of the watermelon was left?

6. Ruth ate $\frac{1}{2}$ of her birthday cake and her sister, Grace, ate $\frac{2}{6}$ of it. Who ate a bigger portion of the cake?

7. My 3 friends and I share a mango pie equally. How many pieces must I cut the pie into so that each of us gets 2 pieces?

8. A fruit-seller cut half a honeydew into 10 equal slices. A customer bought $\frac{1}{2}$ of them. How many slices of honeydew were left?

9. Mrs. Martin bought 8 cartons of strawberry milk. Her children drank $\frac{3}{4}$ of it. How many cartons of strawberry milk did they finish?

10. Father cut a grapefruit into 8 equal slices. He and Mother ate one slice each.

    (a) What fraction of the grapefruit was not eaten?

    (b) What fraction of the grapefruit did they eat?

Take the Challenge!

1. Work out the following problems. Which of the sums is the largest?

    (a) $\dfrac{1}{5} + \dfrac{1}{5} =$

    (b) $\dfrac{1}{2} + \dfrac{1}{4} =$

    (c) $\dfrac{1}{3} + \dfrac{1}{6} =$

    (d) $\dfrac{1}{2} + \dfrac{1}{3} =$

2. Mrs. Martinez ordered a pizza. The boys ate $\frac{2}{5}$ of the pizza while the girls ate $\frac{1}{2}$ of it. One of the boys, Mike, said that all of them ate $\frac{3}{7}$ of the whole pizza. Was Mike correct?

3. I transferred $\frac{1}{2}$ of the jelly beans from Jar A into Jar B. After that there were 96 jelly beans in Jar A and three times as many in Jar B. How many jelly beans were in Jar A and Jar B at first?

4. A grocer filled 1 large bag and 3 small bags with 3 kg of salt. Each small bag contained $\frac{1}{3}$ as much salt as the large bag. How many grams of salt were there in each small bag?

1. Match the time to the correct clock. Write the letter of the answer on top of the question number in the box below to decode the riddle. The first one has been done for you.

(a) 10 minutes past three

(b) A quarter past 1

(c) 15 minutes before 4

(d) 25 minutes past 7

(e) 15 minutes to 8

(f) 40 minutes past 10

(g) 5 minutes before midnight

(h) A quarter to 3

(i) 35 minutes after 5

(j) 20 minutes past 9

T
E
C
J
H
N
U
D
O
S

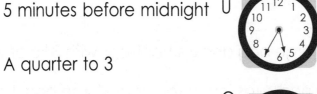

Don't count the minutes at the dining table,
___ ___ ___ ___   ___ ___ __E__   ___ ___ ___ ___ ___ ___ ___ ___
(c) (i) (e) (g)   (g) (b) (a)   (e) (a) (d) (f) (h) (j) (e)

2. Write the beginning and ending time shown on the clocks and complete the time interval between them.

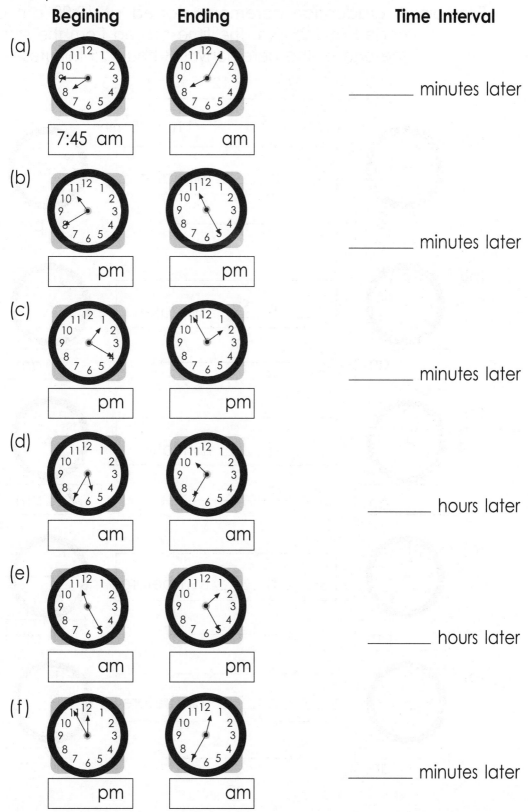

	Begining	**Ending**	**Time Interval**
(a)	7:45 am	am	_____ minutes later
(b)	pm	pm	_____ minutes later
(c)	pm	pm	_____ minutes later
(d)	am	am	_____ hours later
(e)	am	pm	_____ hours later
(f)	pm	am	_____ minutes later

65

3. How many hours and minutes have passed? Fill in the correct answers in the boxes.

Example: A graduation ceremony started at 10:00 am and ended at 1:25 pm. The time passed from the start to the end of the ceremony is 3 hours 25 minutes.

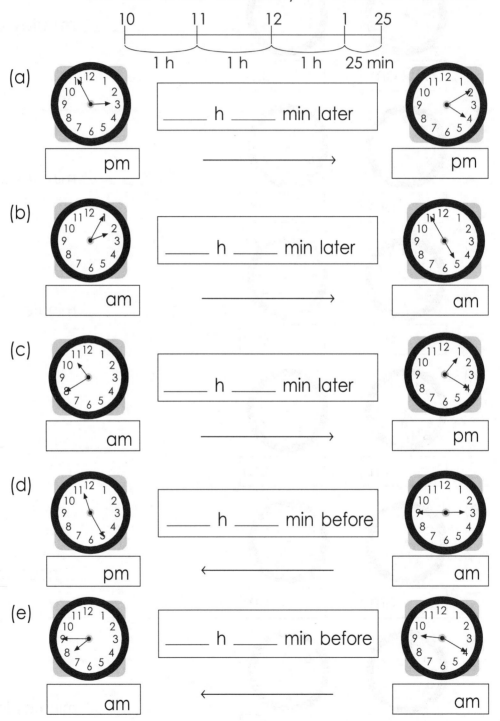

(a) _____ h _____ min later

pm   →   pm

(b) _____ h _____ min later

am   →   am

(c) _____ h _____ min later

am   →   pm

(d) _____ h _____ min before

pm   ←   am

(e) _____ h _____ min before

am   ←   am

66

4. Estimate how long you should take to do the following. Circle the correct answer and write its letter on top of the question number below to solve the riddle. The first one has been done for you.

(a) The time it takes to wash and dry your hands.
    (V) 1 second   (H) 1 minute   (L) 1 hour

(b) How long you spend to watch a movie at the cinema?
    (B) 2 hours   (F) 20 minutes   (J) 2 days

(c) The time you take to say your name.
    (K) 2 minutes   (D) 20 seconds   (S) 2 seconds

(d) The time you take to brush your teeth.
    (E) 3 minutes   (T) 3 seconds   (M) 30 minutes

(e) The time it takes to make a call on the telephone.
    (Q) 5 hours   (X) 5 minutes   (A) 5 seconds

(f) How long each person usually sleeps at night?
    (R) 80 days   (P) 8 years   (Y) 8 hours

(g) The amount of time a student spends on homework at one time.
    (T) 2 hours   (H) 4 minutes   (Z) 4 weeks

(h) The amount of time for a tree to fully grow.
    (W) 6 hours   (V) 6 years   (N) 6 days

(i) The time interval between spring and winter seasons.
    (G) 12 years   (L) 12 weeks   (O) 12 months

(j) The time mother takes to boil an egg.
    (B) 10 seconds   (G) 10 minutes   (W) 10 hours

(k) The time between this birthday and the next.
    (M) 1 year   (U) 1 month   (K) 1 week

What do a computer and a shark have in common?

T __ __ __   __ __ __ __   __ __ __ __
(g) (a) (d) (f)   (b) (i) (g) (a)   (a) (e) (h) (d)

__ __ __ __ __ __ __ __ __
(k) (d) (j) (e) (b) (f) (g) (d) (c)

5. Convert the following into minutes.

    (a) 1 h 15 min = _____ min

    (b) 2 h 55 min = _____ min

    (c) 3 h 25 min = _____ min

    (d) 1 h 40 min = _____ min

6. Convert the following into hours and minutes.

    (a) 80 min = _____ h _____ min

    (b) 105 min = _____ h _____ min

    (c) 215 min = _____ h _____ min

    (d) 275 min = _____ h _____ min

7. Convert the following into seconds.

    (a) 1 min 10 s = _____ s

    (b) 2 min 15 s = _____ s

    (c) 1 min 50 s = _____ s

    (d) 4 min 55 s = _____ s

8. Convert the following into minutes and seconds.

    (a) 95 seconds = _____ min _____ s

    (b) 125 seconds = _____ min _____ s

    (c) 240 seconds = _____ min _____ s

    (d) 315 seconds = _____ min _____ s

9. Convert the following into months.

    (a) 1 year 3 months = _____ months

    (b) 2 years 8 months = _____ months

    (c) 4 years 6 months = _____ months

    (d) 3 years 11 months = _____ months

10. Convert the following into years and months.

   (a) 18 months = _____ year _____ months

   (b) 25 months = _____ years _____ months

   (c) 36 months = _____ years _____ months

   (d) 41 months = _____ years _____ months

11. Convert the following into days.

   (a) 1 week 3 days = _____ days

   (b) 2 weeks 5 days = _____ days

   (c) 3 weeks 3 days = _____ days

   (d) 4 weeks 6 days = _____ days

12. Convert the following into weeks and days.

   (a) 16 days = _____ weeks _____ days

   (b) 30 days = _____ weeks _____ days

   (c) 40 days = _____ weeks _____ days

   (d) 63 days = _____ weeks _____ days

13. Add and subtract in compound units.

   (a) 1 h 15 min + 35 min = _____ h _____ min

   (b) 2 h 40 min + 1 h 35 min = _____ h _____ min

   (c) 3 h 25 min + 1 h 55 min = _____ h _____ min

   (d) 2 h 50 min – 35 min = _____ h _____ min

   (e) 4 h 20 min – 1 h 45 min = _____ h _____ min

   (f) 3 h – 1 h 50 min = _____ h _____ min

14. Look at the signs and answer the questions.

(a) What do you look at to find out which day of the week the Children's Fest begins?

_____

Come to the
CHILDREN'S FEST
May 27 to June 24

Fest Hours
Open: 10:00 am
Close 9:00 pm

Admission Tickets
4 for $10.00

(b) Mrs. Selvam bought $20.00 worth of tickets. How many did she buy?

_____

(c) How long does the Children's Fest last each day?

_____ hours

(d) Mr. Bose is going to take his 4 children together with their mother to the Children's Fest. How much must he pay for their tickets?

$_____

NEXT
PONY
RIDE

(e) It is now 2:45 pm. How many more minutes must Mr Bose's children wait to take the next pony ride?

_____ minutes

(f) For how many days is the Children's Fest open? _____

(g) What time will the next pony ride be at if the pony rides are available every half an hour?

_____ pm

WORD PROBLEMS

1. A train left the station in Town A at half past 7 in the morning. The train arrived in Town B at 2:30 pm. How long did the train take for the journey?

2. It takes 1 hour and 15 minutes to bake a cake. If I put the cake mixture into the oven at 2:20 pm, at what time will it be ready?

3. My computer class starts at 1:45 pm. I am at the computer school now and it is only 1:10 pm. By how many minutes am I early?

4. Ronny went to bed at a quarter to midnight. He slept for 9 hours and 15 minutes. What time did he get up the next day?
Use the time line to help you solve the problem.

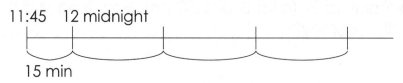

11:45   12 midnight

15 min

5. Vanessa has violin practice from 3:00 pm to 4:15 pm every Wednesday, Friday and Sunday. How many hours and minutes of violin practice does she have in a week?

6. This is Jenani's schedule every Saturday.

10:00 am	English drama class
12:15 pm	Lunch and leisure
3:30 pm	Mathematics tutoring
5:00 pm	Homeward bound

How much longer is her English drama class than her mathematics tutoring lesson?

7. A clock at a train station platform shows 5:55 am. The correct time is 6:15 am. How many minutes is the clock slower?

8. My mother reached home at 7:20 pm. She was 25 minutes later than the usual time. What time does she usually reach home?

9. The time is now 3:05 pm. Aisha took her lunch 3 hours and 15 minutes ago. At what time did Aisha take her lunch?

10. A movie "Knight Time" is screened at a theater at the following times:

    11:30 am, 1:20 pm, 3:10 pm , _____ , 6:50 pm, 8:40 pm

    (a) The time for the 4th show is missing. When should it begin?

    _____

    (b) Nina arrives at the theater half an hour after noon. In how many minutes' time will the next movie start? _____

Take the Challenge!

1. Gywnn bought a clock from Off-Time Clock Company. The clock loses 15 minutes every hour (in other words, it is 15 minutes slow). If Gywnn adjusts the clock and it reads the correct time at 12:00 noon today, what time will it read when the actual time is 6:00 pm in the evening?
   (*Hint*: Make a table to organise the data.)

Actual Time	Gywnn's Time	Minutes Slower
12:00 noon	12:00 noon	0
1:00 pm	12:45 pm	15

2. Zack was born 2 years after Paul was born. Ryan is 4 years older than Zack. Jean is 8 years younger than Ryan. Tess was born a year after Jean. Who is the second oldest?

3. A tap in the toilet is leaking 50 ml of water an hour. Father placed a bucket below it and collected 10,000 ml of water. How long has the tap been leaking? Give your answer in days and hours.
   (*Hint*: There are 24 hours in 1 day.)

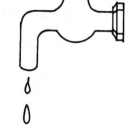

Topic 8: Geometry

1. How many turns or rounds are made in the following?

   (a) When you open a door, do you notice how much of a turn you are making? Is it a whole turn, less than a whole turn or more than a whole turn?

   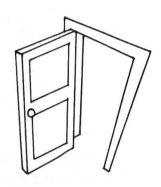

   _____

   (b) Jerry was looking at the aquarium and turned to look at the cat. He made (more than/less than) a whole turn. [Underline the correct answer.]

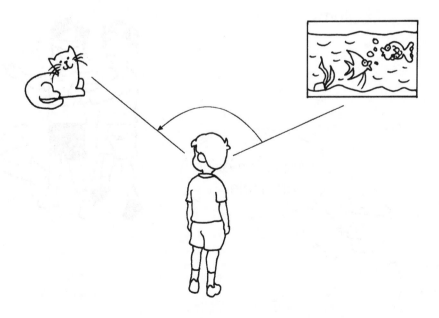

75

(c) When I flip a page of a book, it makes a (whole/half) turn.
[Underline the correct answer.]

(d)

Breakfast was at 7:30 am. Lunch was at 12:30 pm. How many whole turns has the minute hand made between breakfast and lunch? _____ turns

(e) Dennis blindfolded his friend to play a game. Each time Dennis turned his friend around once, he counted one. How many turns did Dennis make if he counted ten?

_____ turns

Turning is making an angle.

2. Rank these angles from the smallest to the largest and fill in their letters in the table below. The first one has been done for you.

(a)

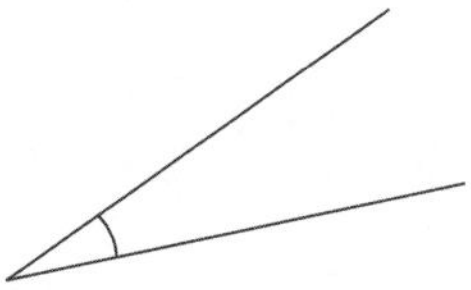

(b)

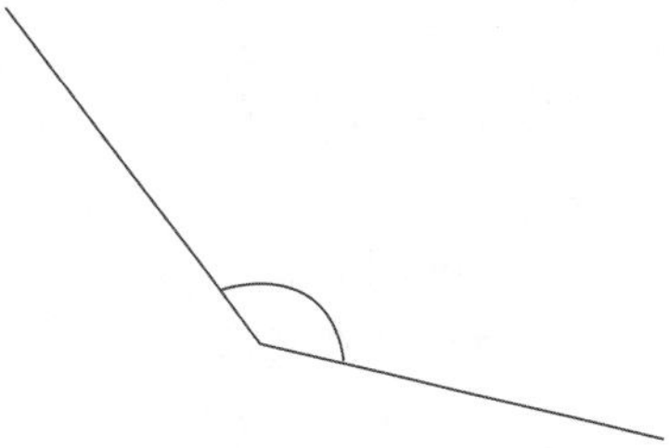

(c)

(d)

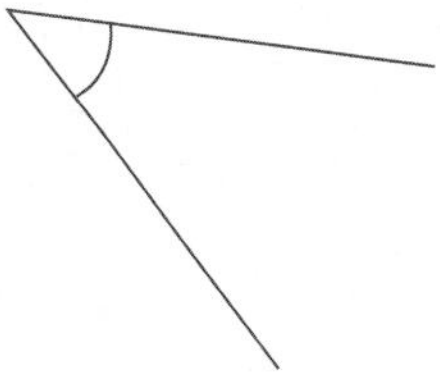

(e)

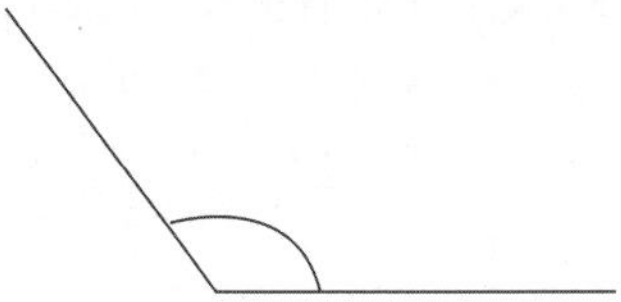

(f)

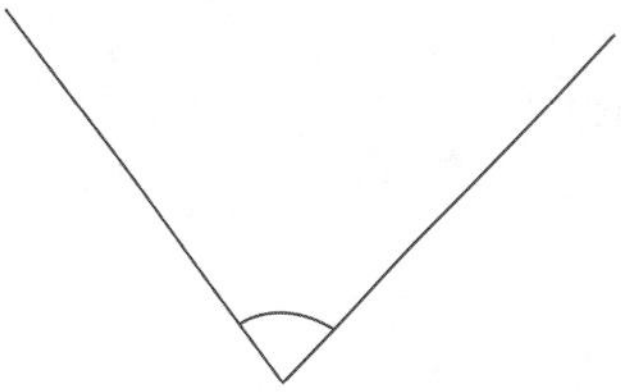

(g)

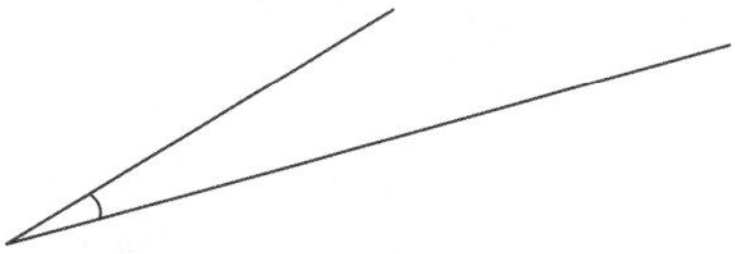

(h)

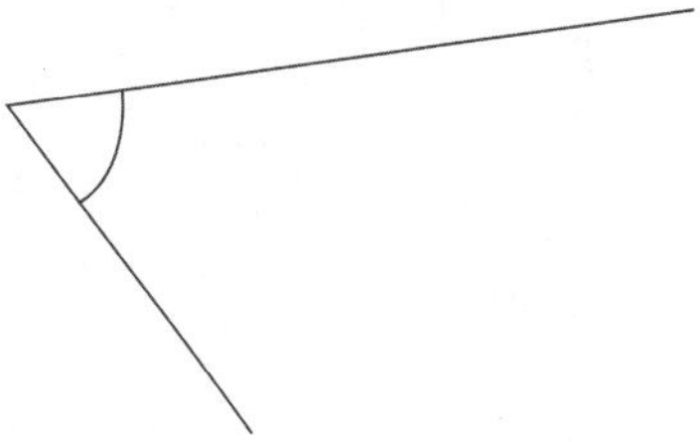

(i)

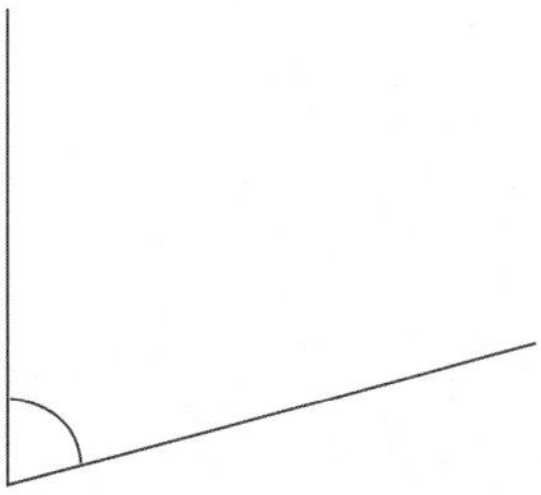

(j)

smallest ———————————————————————→ largest

(g)									

3. Refer to the angles in Question 2. Group them into the following: "less than a right angle", "more than a right angle" or "right angle".

4. How many right angles are there in each of these diagrams?

(a)

(b)

_____

_____

(c)

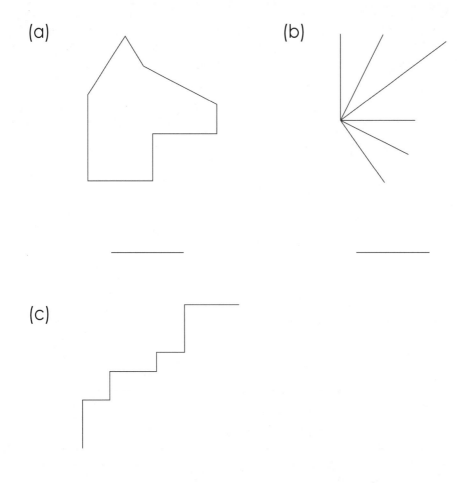

_____

5. Study the figures and complete the table below.

(a)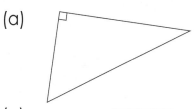

(b)

(c)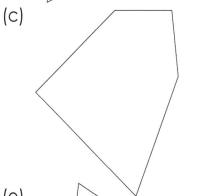

(d)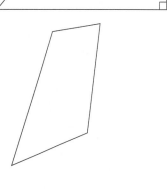

(e)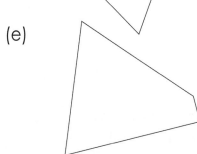

(f)

(g)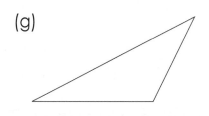

(h)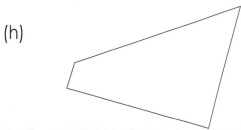

Figure	Number of sides	Total number of angles	Number of angles less than a right angle	Number of angles more than a right angle
(a)				
(b)				
(c)				
(d)				
(e)				
(f)				
(g)				
(h)				

6. Sort out these angles into right angles, angles less than a right angle and angles more than a right angle.

Wow! Every place and thing has angles in them.

Right angles	Angles less than a right angle	Angles more than a right angle

7. What is the similiarity in each of these figures?

_____

_____

8. Mark all the angles in the figure with the letter 'a'.

(a) 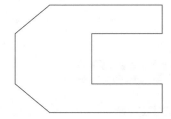   (b)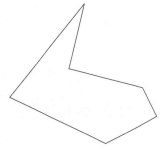

9. What is the sum of the number of angles more than a right angle in these two figures? _____

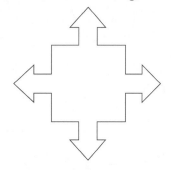

10. Count the number of right angles in the figures below.

(a) 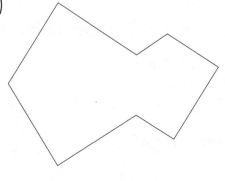   (b)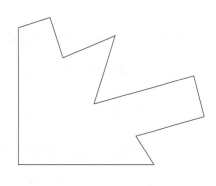

_____   _____

11. Circle the figures that are different from the rest.

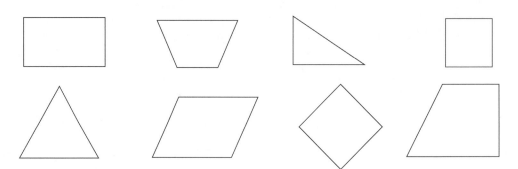

1. List 4 similarities that all these figures have.

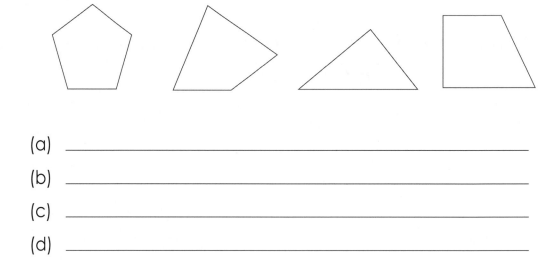

   (a) _____

   (b) _____

   (c) _____

   (d) _____

2. Fold a circle along the dotted lines shown. Open up the circle.

   (a) What fraction of a turn is each part?

   _____

   (b) What fraction of a turn is a right angle?

   _____

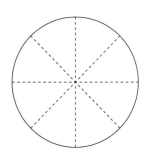

Topic 9: Area and Perimeter

1. How many squares make up each of these shapes?

Remember that two triangles make up one square as shown. The number of squares gives its area.

This is a square unit.

(a)

_____

(b)

_____

(c)

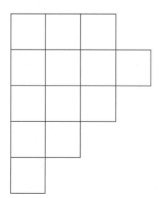

_____

(d)

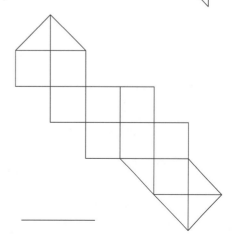

_____

(e) 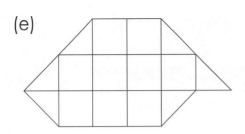   (f)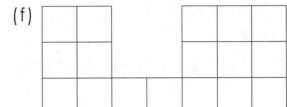

_____   _____

2. (a) Which shape in Question 1 has the largest area? _____

   (b) Which shape has the smallest area? _____

3. Work out the area of these figures in square units.

(a) 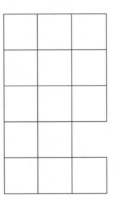   (b)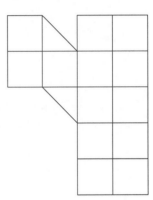

_____   _____

(c) 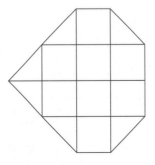   (d)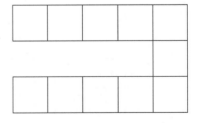

_____   _____

(e)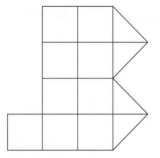

_____

(f)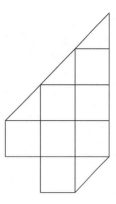

_____

(g)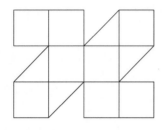

_____

(h)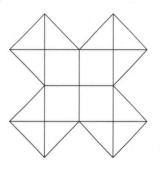

_____

(i)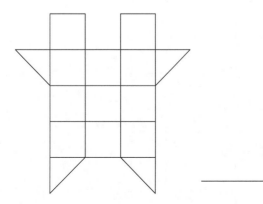

_____

4. Draw on the same grid below the squares indicated. The first one has been done for you.

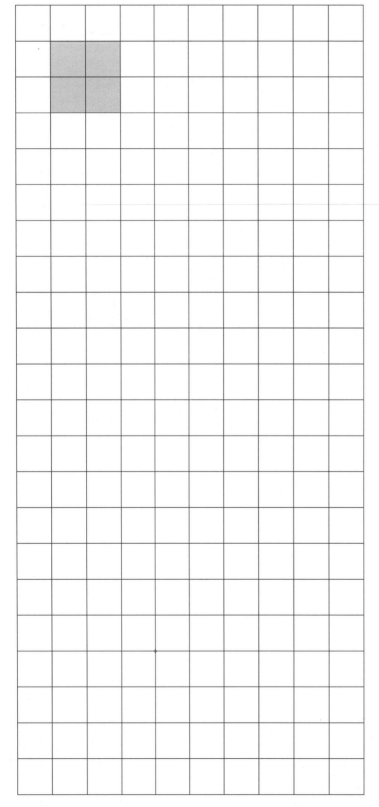

(a) A 2-cm square

Area = _____ cm²

(b) A 4-cm square

Area = _____ cm²

(c) A 6-cm square

Area = _____ cm²

(d) A 9-cm square

Area = _____ cm²

5. What is the area of each figure? On the right grid, draw another figure of the same area.

1 cm

1 cm

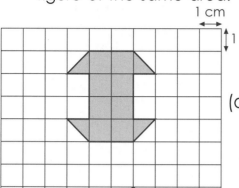

(a) Area =

_____ cm²

(b) Area =

_____ cm²

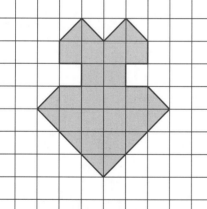

(c) Area =

_____ cm²

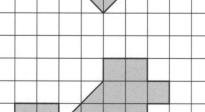

(d) Area =

_____ cm²

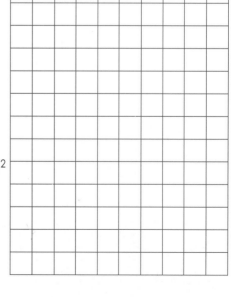

6. Find the perimeter and area of each figure made up of 1-cm squares. Put your answers in the table.

The perimeter of a figure is the total length around it.

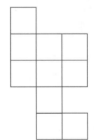

(a)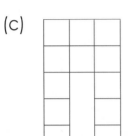

(b)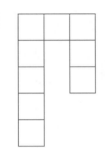

(c)

(d)

(e)

(f)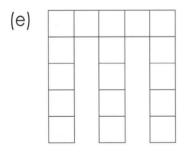

(g)

Figure	(a)	(b)	(c)	(d)	(e)	(f)	(g)
Perimeter in cm							
Area in cm²							

7. (a) Which two figures in Question 6 have the same area and perimeter? _____ and _____

(b) Which two figures in Question 6 have the same area but different perimeter? _____ and _____

(c) Which two figures in Question 6 have the same perimeter but different area? _____ and _____

8. Find the perimeter of each figure and match its answer to the letter in the box on the right to decode the message on the next page.

(a)

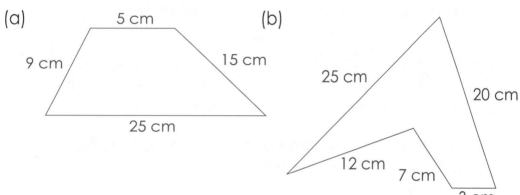

(b)

(c)

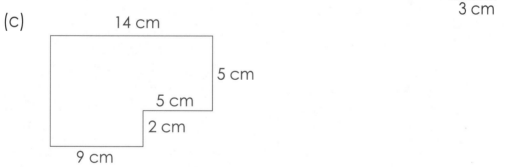

(d)

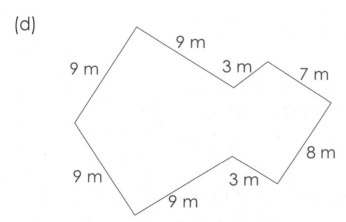

Answers:	
E	67 cm
G	42 cm
L	68 m
H	54 cm
N	50 cm
T	57 m

(e)

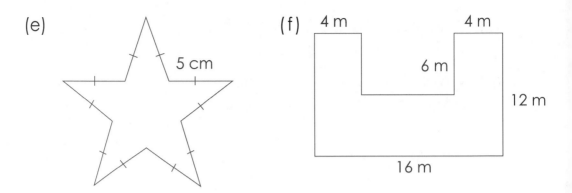

5 cm

(f) 4 m   4 m

6 m

12 m

16 m

The area of a figure measures the amount of space it covers, but the perimeter measures the _____ of its edges.

____   ____   ____   ____   ____   ____
(f)   (b)   (e)   (c)   (d)   (a)

---

9. Find the area and perimeter of each rectangle. Put your answers in the table on the next page.
   Example:

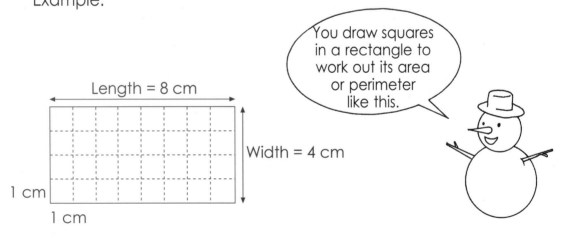

You draw squares in a rectangle to work out its area or perimeter like this.

Length = 8 cm

Width = 4 cm

1 cm

1 cm

There are 4 rows of eight 1-cm squares.
That is,   Area of rectangle = Length × Width
$$= 8 \times 4$$
$$= 32 \text{ cm}^2$$

Perimeter of rectangle = 8 + 8 + 4 + 4
$$= 24 \text{ cm}$$

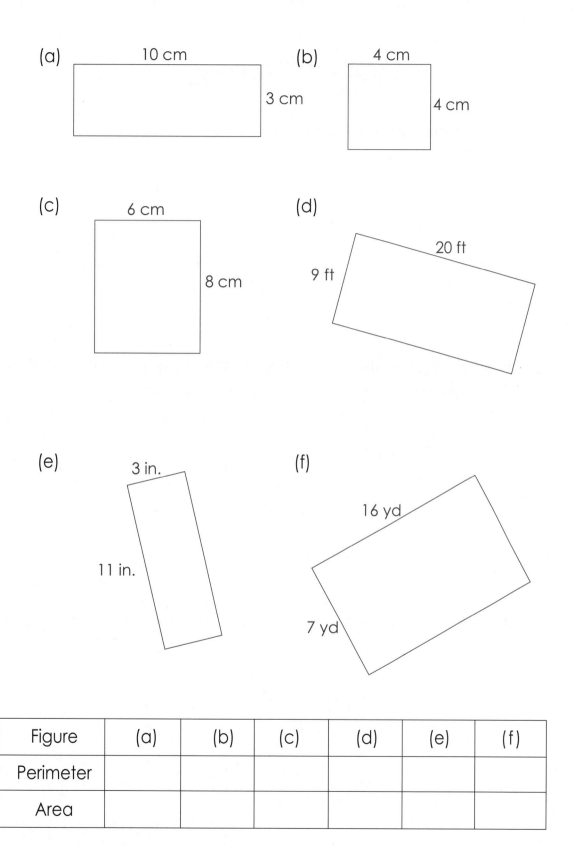

(a) 10 cm, 3 cm

(b) 4 cm, 4 cm

(c) 6 cm, 8 cm

(d) 20 ft, 9 ft

(e) 3 in., 11 in.

(f) 16 yd, 7 yd

Figure	(a)	(b)	(c)	(d)	(e)	(f)
Perimeter						
Area						

* Remember to write the units correctly.

WORD PROBLEMS

1. Find the area of the figure below which is made up of a square and a rectangle.

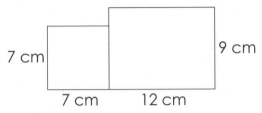

2. By how much is the area of rectangle M greater than that of rectangle N?

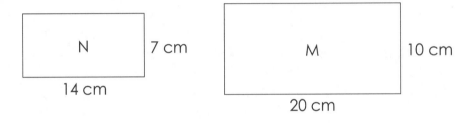

3. What is the total perimeter of the square X and the rectangle Y?

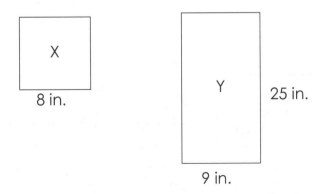

4. Abby used a wire to make a rectangle. It has a length of 45 in. and a width of 10 in. How long is the wire?

5. The figure is made up of a square P and a rectangle Q. The perimeter of square P is 20 cm. Find the area of rectangle Q.

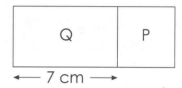

6. What is the total perimeter of the two triangles shown below?

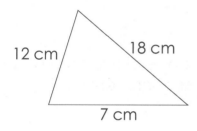
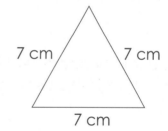

7. The rectangle is divided into similar squares. Find the area and the perimeter of the rectangle.

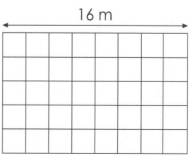

8. The figure is formed with two squares E and F. What is the area of the bigger square F?

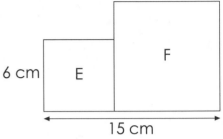

6 cm

E

F

15 cm

9. A rectangular field has a length of 25 yd and a width of 10 yd. Abby ran round it once. How far did she run?

10. The floor of my apartment has the shape of two squares as shown below. What is the perimeter of my apartment?

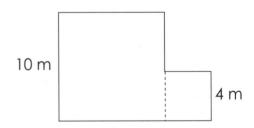

10 m

4 m

Take the Challenge!

1. (a) What fraction of each of these identical squares is shaded?

(i) 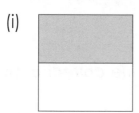   (ii) 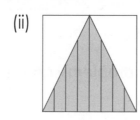   (iii)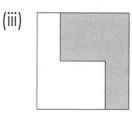

(iv) 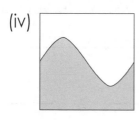   (v)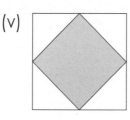

(b) What can you say about the areas of the shaded parts?

2. You are given 4 identical squares. Arrange these 4 squares to touch one another at the corners but not at the sides, so that they are enclosed in a larger square or rectangle.
   (a) How many different ways can you do it?
   (b) What is the largest and the smallest area of the rectangle formed?

   Example: One possible solution gives an area of 9 square units.

End-Of-Year Review

PART 1

Work out the following problems and write the correct answer in the boxes provided.

1. Find the difference between 3680 and 368. Write your answer in words.

2. In the numeral 4833, the digit '8' stands for $8 \times \boxed{}$.

3. What is the missing number in the box?

   $\boxed{} - 1096 = 3941$

4. Convert 4 km 70 m to meters.

   $\boxed{}$ m

5. Complete the number pattern as shown below.

   | 2450 | 2405 | | 2315 | 2270 |

6. How many hundreds are there in 10,000?

7. What fraction of the figure is **not shaded**?

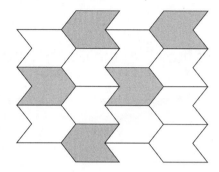

8. $630 \div 7 = 1000 -$ ☐
   Fill in the missing number in the box.

9. What is the product of 261 and 9?

10. Which container holds the most water?

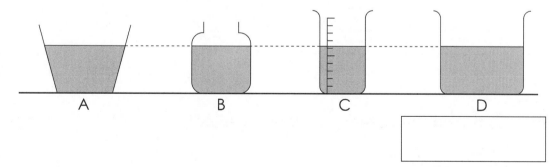

11. A CD-Rom pouch can only hold 8 CDs. I filled up as many such pouches as possible with 68 CDs. How many CDs were in the last pouch?

CDs

12. Jane weighs 60 lb 12 oz. Laura weighs 87 lb 5 oz. How much lighter is Jane than Lara?

lb	oz

13. Which of the diagrams below shows that $\frac{2}{5}$ of the figure is shaded?

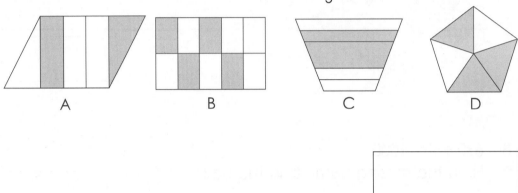

A   B   C   D

14. The same number is missing in the boxes. What is it?

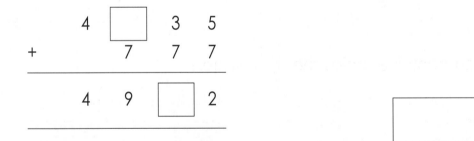

15. Complete the number sentence below.

$$1 - \boxed{} = \frac{4}{7}$$

16. 5635 ml is _____ ℓ _____ ml less than 9 ℓ.

ℓ	ml

98

17.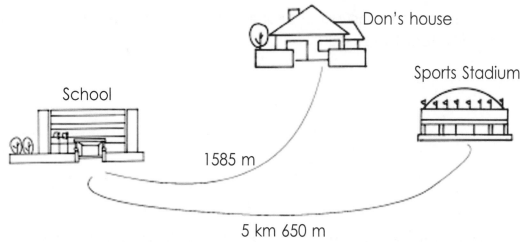

Don's house

Sports Stadium

School

1585 m

5 km 650 m

Don cycled home for lunch and returned to school in the afternoon. Next, he cycled to the Sports Stadium to watch a soccer game. How far did Don cycle in all?

km	m

18. How many quarters can you exchange for a $5 bill?

quarters

19. What is the weight of each crab if they weigh the same?

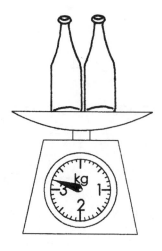

g

20. The figure is made up of similar triangles with sides 2 cm. Find the perimeter of the figure.

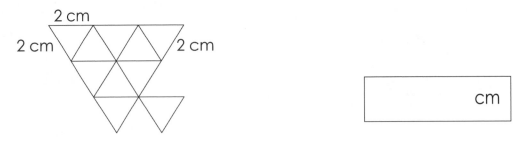

2 cm

2 cm   2 cm

cm

21. How many angles in the figure are less than a right angle?

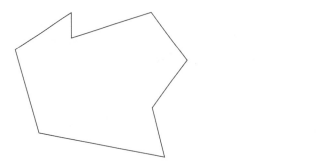

22. Clarice is 6 years 5 months old. Her cousin, Andrew, is 8 months younger. How old is Andrew?

yrs   mths

23. If ✦ + ✦ + ✦ + ☀ + ☀ stands for 34

and ✦ + ☀ stands for 13 , what does ✦ stand for?

24. Mr. Kendrick is 6 ft 1 in. tall. His son, Jeff is 41 in. tall. What is the difference in their height?

ft   in.

25. Look at the letters carefully. Which letters have at least 1 right angle in them?

26. Marina used 450 g of flour to bake a cake. She baked 5 such cakes and still had 200 g of flour left. How much flour did Marina have at first?

kg	g

27.

This is the time on my alarm clock when it rings in the morning. But it is actually 20 minutes slow and I am late for school. What is the actual time?

28. The beaker is already filled with some water. How many full glasses of water can be poured into it before the water in the beaker overflows?

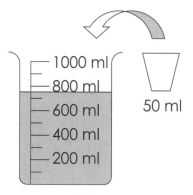

50 ml

glasses

29. Sam has 486 marbles. Aaron has twice as many marbles as Sam. How many marbles do both of them have in total?

marbles

30. Arrange the following fractions from the greatest to the smallest.

$$\frac{4}{9} , \frac{4}{5} , \frac{4}{11}$$

31. The three rectangles P, Q and R are of the same length and width. Which rectangle has the largest shaded area?

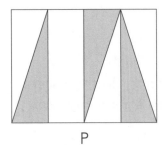 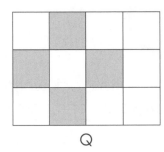 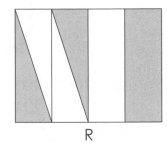

P   Q   R

32. Alice folded 192 paper stars. She folded 6 times as many stars as her sister. How many more paper stars did Alice fold?

more paper stars

33. 5 pens cost $12. Betty bought 20 pens and had $2 left. How much money did she have at first?

$

A group of students in a school was asked to name their favorite snack. Use the graph below to answer Questions 34 and 35.

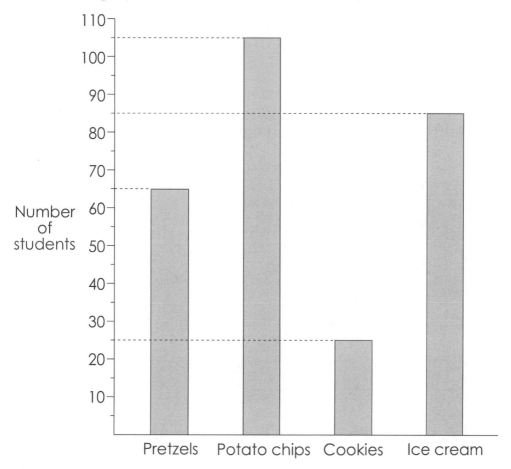

34. How many students were asked to name their favorite snack?

> _____ students

35. What was the most popular snack among the students asked?

> [   ]

36. Abby and her friends bought tickets to watch a movie at 2:15 pm. The movie ended at 3:50 pm. How long did it last?

> _____ h _____ min

37. Write an equivalent fraction of $\frac{2}{3}$.

38. Find the area of the shaded figure.

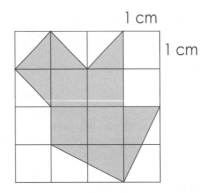

1 cm

1 cm

cm²

39. Mr. Ting bought $\frac{1}{2}$ lb of prawns at \$20 per lb and $\frac{1}{3}$ lb of fresh crab at \$24 per lb. How much did he pay for the prawns and fish altogether?

\$

40. Find the product of all the even numbers between 5 and 11.

PART 2

Show all your work clearly in the space provided.

41. The total cost of a color scanner and a computer chair is $175.00. The computer chair costs $35.20. How much more does the color scanner cost than the computer chair?

42. A rectangular field has a length of 110 m and a width of 55 m. Shawn ran round the field 5 times. What is the total distance Shawn ran? Give your answer in km and m.

43. A waiter mixes 3 qt 2 c of fruit juice with 2 qt 2 c of sparkling wine to make fruit punch. He then pours the fruit punch into 2-quart pitchers. How many pitchers does he need?

44. Mrs. Scampalli baked a large pizza. Her 2 sons ate $\frac{3}{11}$ of the pizza each and her husband ate $\frac{4}{11}$ of the pizza. What fraction of the pizza is left for Mrs. Scampalli?

45. A basket of 7 plums weighs 1 kg 503 g. The empty basket weighs 950 g. How much lighter is a plum than the empty basket?

46. John has his stamp collection in 8 full albums. Each album had 97 stamps in it. He started a new album which has only 6 stamps so far. How many stamps does he have in his collection?

47. Mr. Lim spent $\frac{1}{2}$ of his monthly salary on food and $\frac{1}{3}$ on transport and recreation. He saved the rest. What fraction of his monthly salary did Mr. Lim save?

48. The figure below shows 2 squares A and B and a rectangle C. The 2 squares have the same area. If the perimeter of each square is 16 cm, find the area of the whole figure.

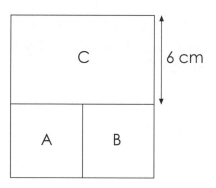

49. Below is a list of some children's programs on a TV channel on a Thursday. Study it carefully and answer the following questions.

10:00 am	Disney's Mickey Mouseworks
11:00	Monster Farm
12:00 noon	Flying Rhino
12:30	The Odyssey
1:35	Sing a Song with Belle
2:00	Animal Planet and Safari
3:25	Newton's Apple

(a) The time is 11:05 am. Mrs. Green is preparing lunch and her children are watching TV. What are they watching?

(b) The children finished lunch and switched on the TV again at 2:15 pm. How much time did they spend watching "Animal Planet and Safari"?

50. Yanni cut a piece of rope 6 m 20 cm long into 3 shorter lengths. The first piece is 3 times as long as the second piece. The second and the third pieces are of equal length. How much longer is the first piece of rope than the second?

More Challenging Problems

1. There are 30 identical beads arranged in a certain order as shown. The beads are either white or black in color.

   (a) What is the color of the 30th bead?
   (b) How many black beads are there?

2. Fill in the boxes with the numbers 1, 3, 5, 7, 9, 11, 13, 15 and 17 such that the sum of the three numbers in the horizontal, vertical and diagonal positions are the same. Each number can only be used once.

3. Samuel filled in the numbers 3, 4, 5, 6, 7, 8, 9, 10 and 11 in the boxes as shown to make the sum of the three numbers in the horizontal, vertical and diagonal postions the same. However, he had filled in two numbers in the wrong boxes. Can you help him to find out what these two numbers are so that their positions can be interchanged to make all the sums equal?

11	5	6
3	7	10
8	9	4

4. In each of the following, each letter represents a number. Can you find out what number each letter represents?

(a)
```
    A  B  C
 +  C  B  A
 _____
 B  B  C  B
 _____
```

A = _____,   B = _____,   C = _____,

(b)
```
    C  D  C
 +  A  B  C
 _____
 A  B  C  D
 _____
```

A = _____,   B = _____,   C = _____,   D = _____

5. Fill in the missing numbers in the boxes for each of the following number patterns.

(a) 5, 11, 23, 47, ⬚ , ⬚

(b) 2, 3, 5, 8, 13, ⬚ , 34, ⬚

(c) 3, 4, 5, 4, 5, 6, 5, 6, 7, ⬚ , ⬚ , ⬚

(d) 2, 3, 5, 8, 12, 17, ⬚ , ⬚

(e) 3, 4, 7, 11, 18, ⬚ , ⬚ , 76

(f) 1, 3, 7, 15, ⬚ , ⬚ , 127

(g) 3, 9, 27, 81, ⬚ , ⬚ , 2187

(h) 1, 4, 9, 16, ⬚ , 36, ⬚ , ⬚ , 81

(i) 1, 2, 8, 48, 384, ⬚ , ⬚

6. Fill in the missing numbers.

(a)

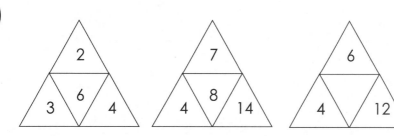

111

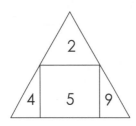
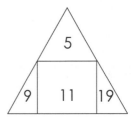
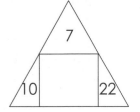

3	5
6	11

7	10
21	31

10	14
40	54

15	20

(c)

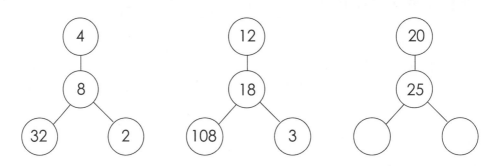

7. Fill in the missing numbers in the two circles.

8. The pages of a book are numbered 1, 2, 3, 4, 5, ... The last page is numbered 146 which has 3 digits. How many digits of all the page numbers are there altogether?

9. Ali, Ben, Caleb and Don are four third graders.
    Ali is taller than Don.
    Don is not the shortest.
    If Ben is the 2nd tallest, who is the tallest and who is the shortest?

10. A, B and C are three numbers such that
    $$A + 6 = B - 6 = 10 + C$$
    Arrange A, B and C in ascending order.

11. A wooden pole is 2 meters long. If it takes 9 seconds to cut the pole once, how long does it take to cut the pole into 8 pieces?

12. Mr. Johnson has his apartment on the sixth floor of a building. He prefers to climb up the stairs when he goes home from work. If there are 16 steps leading to a floor, how many steps does he need to climb in order to reach his floor?

13. A corridor is 30 meters long. Potted plants are placed 5 meters apart on both sides of the corridor from one end to the other end. How many potted plants are there?

14. The diagram shows a clock-face with numbers 1 to 12. Can you divide the clock-face into six equal parts such that the sum of the numbers in each part is the same?

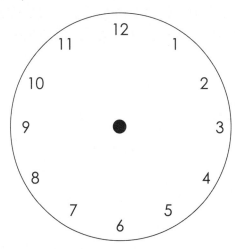

15. In the diagram, five boxes are already filled with numbers. Can you fill in the four missing numbers to make the sum of the three numbers in the horizontal, vertical and diagonal directions the same?

	45	20
35		
	5	40

Answers

Topic 1: Addition and Subtraction (Mental Calculation)

1. (a) 96   (b) 123   (c) 93
   (d) 154   (e) 111   (f) 146
   (g) 101   (h) 138   (i) 132
   (j) 138
2. (a) 97   (b) 179
3. (a) 100   (b) 110   (c) 103
   (d) 101   (e) 141   (f) 82
   (g) 92   (h) 91   (i) 89
   (j) 117
4. (a) 120   (b) 181
5. (a) 173   (b) 144   (c) 162
   (d) 131   (e) 150   (f) 185
   (g) 176   (h) 123   (i) 112
   (j) 144
6. (a) 44   (b) 41   (c) 25
   (d) 32   (e) 75   (f) 32
   (g) 52   (h) 18   (i) 49
   (j) 39
7. (a) 56   (b) 48
8. 47
9. (a) 43   (b) 75   (c) 26
   (d) 12   (e) 23   (f) 11
   (g) 12   (h) 24   (i) 44
   (j) 28
10. (a) 39   (b) 82
11. 72
12. (a) 47   (b) 137   (c) 67
    (d) 34   (e) 153   (f) 87
    (g) 80   (h) 127   (i) 57
    (j) 145
13. (a) 180   (b) 450   (c) 320
    (d) 300   (e) 720   (f) 120
    (g) 1500   (h) 2800   (i) 1800
    (j) 1500   (k) 2100   (l) 3200
14. (a) 490   (b) 1200
15. (a) 40   (b) 40   (c) 20
    (d) 10   (e) 30   (f) 30
    (g) 100   (h) 200   (i) 400
    (j) 50   (k) 300   (l) 400

Word Problems

1. 180   2. 126
3. $480   4. 250
5. $1000   6. 50
7. 4000
8. (a) 1800   (b) 200

9. 180
10. (a) $60   (b) $159

Take the Challenge!

1. $900
2. (a) 80   (b) $480
3. 20

Topic 2: Length

1. (a) 5 in.   (b) 400 yd   (c) 5 cm
   (d) 94 ft   (e) 50 m   (f) 12 ft
2. (a) 185   (b) 645   (c) 927
   (d) 1508   (e) 2617   (f) 1003
3. (a) 1 m 67 cm   (b) 8 m 0 cm
   (c) 4 m 9 cm   (d) 0 m 75 cm
   (e) 15 m 29 cm   (f) 12 m 6 cm
4. (a) 18   (b) 186   (c) 25
   (d) 71   (e) 37   (f) 302
5. (a) 2 yd 1 ft   (b) 26 yd 2 ft
   (c) 16 yd 1 ft   (d) 25 yd 0 ft
   (e) 43 yd 0 ft   (f) 35 yd 1 ft
6. (a) 22   (b) 76   (c) 99
   (d) 44   (e) 35   (f) 123
7. (a) 0 ft 10 in.   (b) 2 ft 1 in.
   (c) 3 ft 4 in.   (d) 4 ft 0 in.
8. (a) equal to   (b) longer than
   (c) shorter than   (d) shorter than
   (e) longer than   (f) longer than
   (g) longer than   (h) equal to
   (i) shorter than   (j) longer than
   (k) shorter than   (l) shorter than
9. (a) 10 m 45 cm; 1 m 45 cm
   (b) 188 m 9 cm; 98 cm
   (c) 2002 cm; 20 cm
   (d) 60 m 5 cm; 5 m 65 cm
   (e) 4 ft; $\frac{1}{2}$ yd
10. (a) 3 m 60 cm   (b) 4 m 90 cm
    (c) 10 m 10 cm   (d) 18 m 82 cm
    (e) 42 m 13 cm   (f) 1 m 11 cm
    (g) 1 m 58 cm   (h) 2 m 8 cm
    (i) 7 m 22 cm   (j) 52 m 72 cm
11. (a) 4 yd 1 ft   (b) 100 yd 0 ft
    (c) 22 yd 1 ft   (d) 9 ft 8 in.
    (e) 38 ft 5 in.   (f) 42 ft 0 in.
    (g) 57 ft 11 in.   (h) 1 yd 0 ft
    (i) 24 yd 1 ft   (j) 2 yd 2 ft
    (k) 7 ft 2 in.   (l) 5 ft 9 in.

(m) 77 ft 9 in.   (n) 97 ft 9 in.
12. (a) 1650   (b) 4108   (c) 9115
    (d) 8028   (e) 6007   (f) 8453
13. (a) 9 km 107 m   (b) 6 km 500 m
    (c) 5 km 47 m   (d) 6 km 6 m
14. (a) longer than   (b) equal to
    (c) longer than   (d) shorter than
    (e) longer than   (f) equal to
    (g) shorter than   (h) longer than
    (i) longer than
15. (a) 5 km 964 m   (b) 3 km 611 m
    (c) 5 km 739 m   (d) 4 km 842 m
    (e) 7 km 282 m   (f) 4 km 766 m
16. (a) 1780   (b) 14 km 90 m
    (c) 15 km 870 m   (d) 3 km 620 m
    (e) 1840

Word Problems
1. B   2. 8 in.
3. 40   4. 1 km 284 m
5. 483 cm   6. 10 yd
7. 15 km 205 m   8. 8 m 82 cm
9. 28 ft. 4 in.   10. 41 in.

Take the Challenge!
1. 10 m 5 cm   2. Mark

Topic 3: Weight
1. (a) 5 kg   (b) 305 g
   (c) 160 lb   (d) 4 kg 200 g
   (e) 2 oz   (f) 1000 lb
2. (a) 2 kg 400 g   (b) 1 kg 300 g
   (c) 5 kg 500 g   (d) 3 kg 700 g
   (e) 0 kg 750 g   (f) 1 lb 10 oz
   (g) 0 lb 14 oz   (h) 0 kg 650 g
3. (a) 1672   (b) 4809   (c) 7053
   (d) 1022   (e) 6008   (f) 3104
4. (a) 0 kg 940 g   (b) 1 kg 58 g
   (c) 4 kg 307 g   (d) 3 kg 148 g
   (e) 9 kg 435 g   (f) 8 kg 6 g
5. (a) 32   (b) 24   (c) 76
   (d) 35   (e) 107   (f) 170
6. (a) 0 lb 12 oz   (b) 1 lb 4 oz
   (c) 2 lb 4 oz   (d) 0 lb 10 oz
7. (a) cross 508 g, circle 8005 g
   (b) circle 2500 g, cross 2 kg 5 g
   (c) circle 10 kg, cross 9 kg 99 g
   (d) cross 971 g, circle 1 kg 971 g
   (e) cross 18 oz, circle 36 oz
8. (a) 100 g   (b) 150 g   (c) 5 lb
   (d) 3   (e) 250
9. (a) 2 kg 600 g   (b) 6 kg 805 g

(c) 6 kg 465 g   (d) 3 kg 410 g
(e) 1 kg 425 g   (f) 2 kg 280 g
10. (a) 3 lb 9 oz   (b) 7 lb 3 oz
    (c) 26 lb 0 oz   (d) 2 lb 13 oz
    (e) 0 lb 14 oz   (f) 14 lb 9 oz
11. (a) 6 kg 270 g   (b) 3 kg 860 g
    (c) 5 kg 25 g   (d) 4 kg 745 g
    (e) 9 kg 210 g   (f) 2 kg 585 g
12. (a) 14   (b) 14 1b 11 oz
    (c) 20 lb 0 oz

Word Problems
1. 4 kg 500 g   2. 150 g   3. 176 lb
4. 104 lb   5. 4450 g   6. 300 g
7. 3 lb 5 oz   8. $33   9. 1 kg 722 g
10. 47 lb

Take the Challenge!
1. Betty   2. 500 g

Topic 4: Capacity
1. (a) 10 ml   (b) 1 pt   (c) 1 quart
   (d) 400 ml   (e) 2 liters   (f) 15 liters
   (g) 5 liters   (h) 125 gallons
2. (a) 200   (b) 1   (c) 250   (d) 15
3. (a) 400 ml   (b) 700 ml   (c) 100 ml
   (d) 600 ml   (e) 750 ml   (f) 250 ml
   (g) 75 ml   (h) 125 ml   (i) 225 ml
   (j) 30 ml   (k) 70 ml   (l) 90 ml
   Learn from your mistakes.
4. (a) 1600   (b) 2755   (c) 3050
   (d) 1950   (e) 4080   (f) 6105
   (g) 2615   (h) 4125   (i) 4005
5. (a) 1 ℓ 835 ml   (b) 1 ℓ 18 ml
   (c) 3 ℓ 607 ml   (d) 4 ℓ 560 ml
   (e) 2 ℓ 375 ml   (f) 7 ℓ 2 ml
   (g) 4 ℓ 100 ml   (h) 4 ℓ 720 ml
   (i) 4 ℓ 150 ml
6. (a) 7   (b) 9   (c) 14
   (d) 16   (e) 44   (f) 18
   (g) 13   (h) 45   (i) 30
7. (a) 1 gal 3 qt   (b) 1 gal 2 qt
   (c) 4 pt 1 c   (d) 3 qt 1 pt
   (e) 11 qt 1 c   (f) 35 qt 1 pt
   (g) 6 gal 1 qt   (h) 3 gal 2 qt
   (i) 11 qt 1 c
8. (a) 2 ℓ 625 ml   (b) 5 ℓ 160 ml
   (c) 7 ℓ 478 ml   (d) 3 ℓ 190 ml
   (e) 1 ℓ 230 ml   (f) 3 ℓ 150 ml
9. (a) 5 ℓ 900 ml   (b) 875 ml
   (c) 9 ℓ 330 ml   (d) 4 ℓ 776 ml

(e) 6 ℓ 864 ml   (f) 5 ℓ 134 ml

10. (a) 1 gal 2 qt   (b) 18 gal 1 qt
    (c) 600 gal 0 qt   (d) 3 gal 1 pt
    (e) 11 qt 2 c   (f) 7 qt 1 c
    (g) 2 gal 1 qt   (h) 3 gal 2 qt
    (i) 82 gal 3 qt   (j) 3 pt 1 c
    (k) 1 qt 3 c   (l) 3 qt 3 c

11. (a) 10   (b) 950
    (c) 4 ℓ 100 ml

Word Problems

1. 668 ml   2. 7 qt 2 c
3. 6 ℓ 350 ml   4. 7 gal 2 qt
5. 26 qt   6. 2 ℓ 410 ml
7. 12 gal   8. 2230 ml
9. 7 quarts   10. $320

Take the Challenge!

1. (a) 9000 bottles   (b) 4500
2. 800 ml   3. 5   4. 2

Topic 5: Graphs

1. (a) 4   (b) 3   (c) 18
    (d) 14   (e) 1

2. (a) Mice – draw 2, kittens – draw $3\frac{1}{2}$

    (b) 2   (c) 5   (d) Puppies

    (e) 3   (f) $2142   (g) $2\frac{1}{2}$ kg

3. (a) Yes   (b) 12   (c) 1
    (d) $48   (e) 3   (f) 2

4. (a) 45   (b) 18   (c) Leonard
    (d) Cecil   (e) Cecil
    (f) Esther, Cecil

5. (a) 6   (b) orange   (c) 14
    (d) 66   (e) apple   (f) 36
    (g) lemon juice

6. (a) B+   (b) 80   (c) 50   (d) A+, B+
    (e) 130   (f) 350   (g) 10

7. (a) August, July   (b) 1250
    (c) 160   (d) $2640
    (e) 565

Take the Challenge!

2. Reading – 50,
    Talk on Phone – 45,
    Listen to Music – 55,
    Watch TV – 90,
    Surf the Net – 60,
    Play Computer Games – 120

Topic 6: Fractions

1.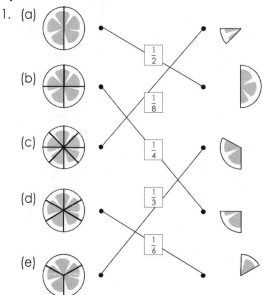

2. (a) (i) $\frac{4}{10}$ (ii) $\frac{6}{10}$ (b) (i) $\frac{3}{8}$ (ii) $\frac{5}{8}$

   (c) (i) $\frac{4}{9}$ (ii) $\frac{5}{9}$ (d) (i) $\frac{2}{8}$ (ii) $\frac{6}{8}$

   (e) (i) $\frac{2}{4}$ (ii) $\frac{2}{4}$ (f) (i) $\frac{2}{6}$ (ii) $\frac{4}{6}$

   (g) (i) $\frac{7}{12}$ (ii) $\frac{5}{12}$ (h) (i) $\frac{4}{8}$ (ii) $\frac{4}{8}$

   (i) (i) $\frac{3}{10}$ (ii) $\frac{7}{10}$ 3. one whole

4. (a) $\frac{1}{2}$ (b) $\frac{1}{3}$ (c) $\frac{1}{2}$

   (d) $\frac{1}{6}$ (e) $\frac{1}{3}$ (f) $\frac{2}{3}$

5. (a) 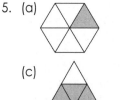   (b)

   (c)   (d)

   (e) 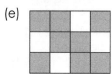   (f)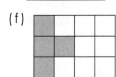

(g)   (h)

6. (a) A, $\frac{1}{7}$ (b) R, $\frac{3}{4}$ (c) 0, $\frac{4}{7}$

   (d) I, $\frac{1}{8}$ (e) U, 1 whole

   (f) N, $\frac{1}{5}$ (g) S', $\frac{4}{9}$ (h) C, $\frac{5}{12}$

   (i) T, $\frac{5}{9}$ (j) F, $\frac{6}{6}$

   (k) FRACTION'S FUN

7. (a) $\frac{1}{5}$ (b) $\frac{8}{9}$

8. (a) $\frac{1}{11}$ (b) $\frac{3}{8}$

9. (a) $\frac{1}{12}$, $\frac{1}{9}$, $\frac{1}{5}$ (b) $\frac{4}{11}$, $\frac{4}{8}$, $\frac{4}{5}$

   (c) $\frac{2}{10}$, $\frac{2}{5}$, $\frac{3}{3}$

10. (a) $\frac{1}{3}$, $\frac{1}{6}$, $\frac{1}{11}$ (b) $\frac{7}{9}$, $\frac{6}{9}$, $\frac{3}{9}$

    (c) $\frac{3}{3}$, $\frac{3}{7}$, $\frac{3}{10}$

11. (a) $\frac{1}{2}$

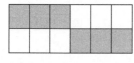

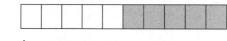

    (b) $\frac{1}{4}$

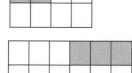

(c) $\frac{1}{3}$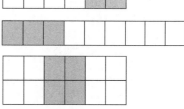

(d) $\frac{3}{4}$

(e) $\frac{2}{3}$

12. (a) C   (b) H   (c) I   (d) P
    (e) M   (f) U   (g) N   (h) K
    CHIPMUNK

Word Problems

1. $\frac{2}{5}$ 2. $\frac{3}{10}$ 3. $\frac{6}{9}$ 4. 2

5. $\frac{7}{12}$ 6. Ruth   7. 8   8. 5

9. 6   10. (a) $\frac{6}{8}$ (b) $\frac{2}{8}$

Take the Challenge!

1. (a) $\frac{2}{5}$ (b) $\frac{3}{4} = \frac{9}{12}$

   (c) $\frac{3}{6}$ (d) $\frac{5}{6} = \frac{10}{12}$ (largest)

2. $\frac{2}{5} + \frac{1}{2} = \frac{4}{10} + \frac{5}{10} = \frac{9}{10}$; No.

3. 192 each   4. 500 g

119

Topic 7: Time

1. (a) E   (b) H   (c) J   (d) C
   (e) S   (f) O   (g) T   (h) N
   (i) U   (j) D
   JUST THE SECONDS
2. (a) 8:05 am; 20
   (b) 10:40 pm, 11:25 pm; 45
   (c) 1:20 pm, 1:55 pm; 35
   (d) 5:35 am, 10:35 am; 5
   (e) 11:25 am, 1:25 pm; 2
   (f) 11:55 pm, 12:35 am; 40
3. (a) 2:55 pm, 1 h 15 min later, 4:10 pm
   (b) 2:05 am, 2 h 50 min later, 4:55 am
   (c) 10:40 am, 2 h 40 min later, 1:20 pm
   (d) 11:25 pm, 3 h 20 min before,
       2:45 am
   (e) 7:45 am, 1 h 35 min before,
       9:20 am
4. (a) H   (b) B   (c) S   (d) E
   (e) A   (f) Y   (g) T   (h) V
   (i) O   (j) G
   (k) M; THEY BOTH HAVE MEGABYTES
5. (a) 75   (b) 175   (c) 205   (d) 100
6. (a) 1, 20 (b) 1, 45 (c) 3, 35 (d) 4, 35
7. (a) 70   (b) 135   (c) 110   (d) 295
8. (a) 1, 35 (b) 2, 5 (c) 4, 0 (d) 5, 15
9. (a) 15   (b) 32   (c) 54   (d) 47
10. (a) 1, 6 (b) 2, 1 (c) 3, 0 (d) 3, 5
11. (a) 10   (b) 19   (c) 24   (d) 34
12. (a) 2, 2 (b) 4, 2 (c) 5, 5 (d) 9, 0
13. (a) 1, 50 (b) 4, 15 (c) 5, 20 (d) 2, 15
    (e) 2, 35 (f) 1, 10
14. (a) calendar (b) 8   (c) 11
    (d) $15.00   (e) 15   (f) 29
    (g) 3:30 pm

Word Problems

1. 7 hours   2. 3:35 pm
3. 35 minutes   4. 9 am
5. 3 h 45 min   6. 45 min longer
7. 20 min slow   8. 6:55 pm
9. 11:50 am
10. (a) 5:00 pm   (b) 50 minutes

Take the Challenge!

1. 4:30 pm   2. Paul
3. 8 days 8 hours

Topic 8: Geometry

1. (a) less than a whole turn
   (b) less than

(c) half   (d) 5   (e) 10
2. (g), (a), (d), (h), (f), (i), (j), (e), (b), (c)
3. Less Than A Right Angle: (a), (d), (f), (h),
   (g), (i);
   More Than A Right Angle: (b), (c), (e);
   A Right Angle: (j)
4. (a) 3   (b) 3   (c) 7
5. (a) 3, 3, 2, 0   (b) 4, 4, 1, 2
   (c) 5, 5, 1, 3   (d) 4, 4, 2, 2
   (e) 4, 4, 2, 1   (f) 4, 4, 0, 0
   (g) 3, 3, 2, 1   (h) 4, 4, 1, 1
6. Right angles: (c), (d), (e)
   Angles less than a right angle: (a), (f)
   Angles more than a right angle: (b), (g)
7. The number of sides equals the number of
   angles in each figure.
8. (a) There should be 10 of them.
   (b) There should be 6 of them.
9. 19
10. (a) 4   (b) 4
11. Circle the 2 triangles.

Take the Challenge!

1. (a) They all have straight lines.
   (b) They all have angles.
   (c) They are 2-dimensional.
   (d) They are enclosed figures.

2. (a) $\frac{1}{8}$ (b) $\frac{1}{4}$

Topic 9: Area and Perimeter

1. (a) 10   (b) 11   (c) 13
   (d) 12   (e) 12   (f) 17
2. (a) f   (b) a
3. (a) 14   (b) 14   (c) 11
   (d) 11   (e) 11   (f) 9
   (g) 10   (h) 10   (i) 13
4. (a) 4   (b) 16   (c) 36   (d) 81
5. (a) 10 (b) 16 (c) 22 (d) 20
6. (a) 18, 12   (b) 24, 11   (c) 22, 12
   (d) 20, 9   (e) 36, 17   (f) 18, 10
   (g) 20, 9
7. (a) d, g   (b) a, c   (c) a, f
8. (a) 54 cm : H   (b) 67 cm : E
   (c) 42 cm : G   (d) 57 cm : T
   (e) 50 cm : N
   (f) 68 cm : L; LENGTH
9. (a) 26 cm, 30 cm^2 (b) 16 cm, 16 cm^2
   (c) 28 cm, 48 cm^2 (d) 58 ft, 180 ft^2
   (e) 28 in., 33 in.^{2} (f) 46 yd, 112 yd^2

Word Problems

1. 157 cm²   2. 102 cm²
3. 100 in.   4. 110 in.
5. 35 cm²   6. 58 cm
7. 160 m², 52 m   8. 81 cm²
9. 70 yd   10. 48 m

Take the Challenge!

1. (a) (i) $\frac{1}{2}$ (ii) $\frac{1}{2}$ (iii) $\frac{1}{2}$

        (iv) $\frac{1}{2}$ (v) $\frac{1}{2}$

   (b) They are equal.
2. Largest: 16 square units; Smallest: 8 square units

End-Of-Year Revew

Part 1

1. Three thousand, three hundred twelve
2. 100   3. 5037   4. 4070
5. 2360   6. 100   7. $\frac{9}{14}$
8. 910   9. 2349   10. D
11. 4   12. 26 lb 9 oz
13. B   14. 1   15. $\frac{3}{7}$
16. 3 ℓ 365 ml   17. 8 km 820 m
18. 20   19. 400
20. 24   21. 2
22. 5 yrs 9 mths   23. 8
24. 2 ft 8 in.   25. Y, H
26. 2 kg 450 g   27. 7:05 am
28. 5   29. 1458
30. $\frac{4}{5}$, $\frac{4}{9}$, $\frac{4}{11}$ 31. R
32. 160   33. 50
34. 280   35. Potato chips
36. 1 h 35 min
37. $\frac{4}{6}$ or $\frac{6}{9}$ or $\frac{8}{12}$
38. 8   39. 18
40. 480

Part 2

41. $104.60 more
42. 1 km 650 m
43. 3   44. $\frac{1}{11}$
45. 871 g lighter   46. 782
47. $\frac{1}{6}$ 48. 80 cm²
49. (a) Monster Farm
     (b) 1 h 10 min
50. 2 m 48 cm longer

More Challenging Problems

1. (a)

	No. of beads
1st group ○●	2
2nd group ○●●	3
3rd group ○●●●	4
4th group ○●●●●	5
5th group ○●●●●●	6
6th group ○●●●●●●	7
	27

After the 6th group, the next 3 beads are ○●● .
The 30th bead is a black one.

   (b) No. of white beads = 6 + 1
                       = 7
      No. of black beads = 30 − 7
                        = 23

2. One possible solution is:

3	17	7
13	9	5
11	1	15

3. The 2 numbers are 10 and 11.
4. (a) B must be 1 because A + C in the hundreds place must be between 10 and 19 inclusive.

```
    A  1  C
+   C  1  A
_____
 1  1  C  1
```

C + A in the ones place must be 11. So C in the tens place must be 3.

```
    A  1  3
+   3  1  A
_____
 1  1  3  1
```

A must be 8.
A = 8, B = 1, C = 3

(b) A must be 1.
    C in the hundreds place must be 9.

```
      9  D  9
  +   1  B  9
  ─────────────
   1  B  9  D
```

B in the hundreds place must be 0.

```
      9  D  9
  +   1  0  9
  ─────────────
   1  0  9  D
```

D must be 8.
A = 1, B = 0, C = 9, D = 8

5. (a) 95, 191   (b) 21, 55
   (c) 6, 7, 8   (d) 23, 30
   (e) 29, 47   (f) 31, 63
   (g) 243, 729   (h) 25, 49, 64
   (i) 3840, 46,080

6. (a)

(b)

(c)

7.

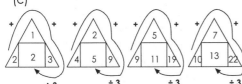

8. Page numbers   No. of digits
   1–9   9
   10–99   90 × 2 = 180
   100–146   47 × 3 = 141
                        330 digits

9.

	1st	2nd	3rd	4th
	(tallest)			(shortest)
Ali	✓			
Ben		✓		
Caleb				✓
Don			✓	✗

Ali cannot be the 3rd tallest as Don is not the shortest. Hence Ali must be the tallest. Since Don is not the shortest he must be the 3rd tallest and Caleb is the shortest.

10. A + 6 = 10 + C
   A + 6 = 4 + C + 6
   A must be bigger than C.
   A + 6 = B – 6
   A + 12 – 6 = B – 6
   B must be bigger than A.
   Ascending order: B, A, C

11. 9 × (8 – 1) = 63 seconds

12. 16 × (6 – 1) = 16 × 5 = 80 steps

13.

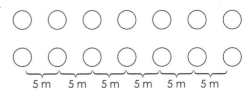

(30 ÷ 5 + 1) × 2 = (6 + 1) × 2
                  = 7 × 2
                  = 14 potted plants

14. 1 + 2 + 3 + 4 + 5 + 6 + 7 + 8 + 9 + 10 + 11 + 12 = 78
   78 ÷ 6 = 13

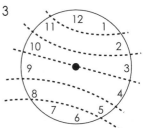

15.

10	45	20
35	25	15
30	5	40